Church
Multiplication
Guide

Church Multiplication Guide

HELPING CHURCHES TO REPRODUCE LOCALLY AND ABROAD

George Patterson and Richard Scoggins

William Carey Library
Pasadena, California

Published by
William Carey Library
1705 N. Sierra Bonita Ave
Pasadena, California 91104
(818) 798-0819

Library of Congress Cataloging-in-Publication Data

Patterson, George, 1932-
    Church multiplication guide : helping churches to reproduce
locally and abroad / George Patterson and Richard Scoggins.
        p.   cm.
    ISBN 0-87808-245-X
    1. Church development, New.   I. Scoggins, Richard.   II. Title.
BV652.24.P36   1994
254′ . 1—dc20   93-40678
                                                                CIP

Scripture taken from the HOLY BIBLE, NEW INTERNATIONAL VERSION. Copyright 1973, 1978, 1984 International Bible Society. Used by permission of Zondervan Bible Publishers.

Art work by Miguel Dubon and George Patterson

Printed in the United States of America

Contents

89980

About the Authors and their Purpose

George Patterson planted churches with the Conservative Baptists for over twenty years in Central America, and since then has coached church planters in different cultures. He began training pastors in a traditional, resident Bible Institute, with poor results. With the help of more experienced missionaries and painful trial and error, he finally saw church multiplication through the instrumentality of "Theological Education *and* Evangelism by Extension" (TEEE). This non-formal pastoral training resulted in twenty years in about 100 new churches in northern Honduras. The model is being adapted to fields in Asia, Africa and throughout Latin America, as well as by churches in the United States. George serves as a coach to those who seek church reproduction--daughter churches, granddaughter churches, etc.--by using sound biblical discipling principles. His experiences coaching church planting teams and trainers during the last eight years have convinced him that the principles of church reproduction need wider exposure, which has led him to join Dick Scoggins in writing this *Church Multiplication Guide.*

"Our main objective in writing this guide," George explains, "is to see *churches reproduce churches.* We pray that this book will strengthen your vision and resolve to enable your church (or the church of your disciples) to multiply itself locally and in unevangelized fields. Pray also for God's help to envision your church reproducing "daughter" and "granddaughter" churches. If your church has small home fellowships or discipling groups, pray that he may help you envision these multiplying also.

"We emphasize church *multiplication* as well as the more common term *church planting* because church growth by multiplication is more strategic and biblical than growth by addition *only.* Growth by addition, as in Acts 2:41, usually extracts converts from a definite extended social circle, drawing them into a new circle, the church. In growth by multiplication, as in Acts chapters 10-16, the church penetrates other social circles, near and far, and reproduces itself inside the converts' networks of relatives and friends. This multiplies the nuclei around which addition more easily takes place, leading to exponential increase. It is practiced more commonly by non-Western churches."

For information: *Church Planting International, 9521-A Business Center Dr., Cucamonga, CA 91730, USA; (909) 945 1264.*

Richard Scoggins coordinates the Fellowship of Church Planters. He came to Christ through Quidnessett Baptist Church, Providence, R.I., which had the goal to reproduce new churches. He immediately became involved. His first effort, the Cranston Christian Fellowship, followed a centralized, large group church model and emphasized spiritual healing and personal discipleship focused on Christ as the model for character development. He says, "During this time I learned by personal experience that God provides leaders from a congregation's midst, as we combine opportunities for service with practical training."

Richard was later sent with a team to plant the Warwick Christian Fellowship where, as he says, "I realized the benefits of plural eldership, as opposed to what I was still modeling--a one-man pastorate with a supporting board. I asked the church to commission me as part of a team of men to do church planting and we formed the Fellowship of Church Planters.

"The new church soon plateaued; we seemed no closer to establishing spontaneously reproducing churches than we had been thirteen years earlier, except that we had the vision. About this time, George Patterson became our coach and helped us see that those we discipled had to pass on the torch. He helped us to focus more on the second and third generations of discipleship, as in 2 Timothy 2:2.

"We started a house church in rural Rhode Island and became aware of the "family" dynamics of the small house church life, where individuals can give and receive love and healing, and the crippling effects of sin are more easily brought to light. We told each other, 'You can run, but you can't hide. And if you run, we will run after you!'"

Since then Richard has affirmed, "We have seen God raise up new leaders at an extraordinary rate and house churches reproduce into house church networks. George challenged us to reproduce church planting teams in other metropolitan areas. So we have formed the Fellowship of Church Planting Teams, an alliance of teams and churches committed to reproduce disciples and networks of new churches and church planting teams. It has already produced church planting teams in the Boston and Los Angeles areas."

For information: *Fellowship of Church Planting Teams, 75 Capron Dr., Warwick, RI 02886.*

Church Multiplication Guide

Introduction

1. The simplicity of church multiplication (trust in God's power).

Does church multiplication sound hard? Does the idea of your church reproducing itself seem "way out" to you? Perhaps we need to expose a myth. You may have heard a whisper just now as we raised this topic: "Church multiplication sounds nice, but in this sophisticated age it requires a lot of money, specialized education, sophisticated organization, high-powered executive leadership, and costly buildings." Well, you can whisper back this fact: Churches multiply more readily precisely where these things are lacking. Actually, churches that reproduce do not rely on these things for their reproduction.

Basically, church multiplication comes from our love for Christ and the resulting desire to obey his command to disciple all peoples or ethnic groups. A church makes the sacrifice in love to prepare, separate, and hold responsible those members with the "apostolic" gift for planting churches in another culture. But members with many other spiritual gifts and ministries cooperate in the power of the Holy Spirit to make this possible.

Another myth about church multiplication that we should explode is that it works only in certain cultures (rural, urban, tribal, village, in China or Korea, etc.). The two authors of this guide, George Patterson and Richard Scoggins, bring examples of church multiplication from the two ends of the cultural spectrum, so your church ought to fall somewhere in between. Patterson worked with rural, poor, uneducated Hondurans in a pioneer field; Scoggins works among urban, educated, affluent, middle-class Americans in the shadow of the oldest Baptist church in the world and the oldest synagogue in the United States (in Providence and Newport, Rhode Island).

Space does not permit listing all the examples of spontaneous church multiplication among Muslims, tribal peoples, Chinese, Burmese, Cubans, Nepalese, Texans, and many others. This church multiplication by God's power can happen wherever we find good soil for real church growth. "Good soil" for growth through conversion is bad people (Rom. 5:20)! Some peoples are indeed more responsive than others, but church multiplication is happening to some degree within every major category of people groups. God will use your gift-based ministry to help do it.

Help your church to reproduce through *ongoing* renewal. The Holy Spirit multiplies churches in movements called "renewal," "revival," "restoration," or "outpouring of the Holy Spirit"--if we let him continually renew us *day by day* (not just a temporary experience, 2 Cor. 4:16), *and* if we enable all members to do their different ministries, *and* if we do not center the renewal around one spiritual gift. Apostate and stagnant churches are renewed by the Holy Spirit as they begin again to pray and glorify Jesus Christ. This renewal, however, is often limited by us. It may improve only our teaching. Or members' lives are transformed as they begin praying in the Spirit, using the gift of tongues, with only a temporary effect on the outreach of the church. A thoroughgoing, ongoing renewal releases *all* the gifts given to a particular

---

> **Record items you plan to deal with later** in Appendix E *Items to Review.* Mark the box ☐ by the item's number in Appendix E which lists all numbered subtitles. Discuss them later with your coworkers and plan accordingly.

church body. The Holy Spirit will separate those with the apostolic (missionary) gift to multiply the church (Acts 13:1-3). This requires the sacrificial cooperation of all gift-based ministries, out of love for Christ and each other (not out of guilt, ambition, or merely a desire to reach goals or chase a vision). Unfortunately, many with this apostolic gift go outside of their church body to seek preparation, to have their gift recognized, and to be held accountable for church multiplication. Their own church may perhaps merely "commission" them, pray, and send money. Teachers and leaders in such a fractured body seldom use their gifts to prepare and mobilize those with the apostolic gift; the church fails to reproduce itself consciously and purposefully through them in the power of the Holy Spirit.

2. Define and keep in mind your ministry, and that of your co-workers, as you use this *Guide.*

This Church Multiplication Guide is used by people with very different responsibilities. For it to be most helpful to you, please define as best you can your main ministry—now or expected in the future. To help you keep it in mind as you work through the book, mark your ministry category(ies) in the box below. Keep in mind also the ministries of your colleagues; form your plans not as an individual working alone but in harmony with your coworkers whose ministries and gifts balance yours. Church multiplication skills are acquired by working with others as a body—not from lectures or books, including this guide. Using this book by yourself will not help you multiply churches; it requires teamwork.

Mark the following categories that correspond *closest* to your probable career work. Include voluntary or part-time ministries. If unsure, mark the last box under an item; do not make a premature decision.

Ministry Categories

If *evangelism* or *witnessing for Jesus* is your main ministry, mark how:
- ☐ witnessing for Jesus with a church planting team
- ☐ witnessing with an established church or churches
- ☐ independent preaching (not with a church planting team or a specific church)
- ☐ This decision depends on further information.

If *planting churches* is your main ministry, where?
- ☐ in a pioneer field (one that lacks obedient, reproductive churches)
- ☐ in a distant field that already has churches but needs more
- ☐ locally, with my own people or ethnic group
- ☐ locally, with a different ethnic group (cross-culturally)
- ☐ This depends on further information.

If *pastoring* is your main ministry, with whom?
- ☐ a congregation, as "senior" pastor (or coordinator of the elders)
- ☐ a congregation, as an associate pastor, worship leader, youth pastor, missions pastor, etc.
- ☐ a small group, as a shepherd or pastor-teacher
- ☐ persons who need counseling or personal discipling, as a mentor, adviser, counselor, tutor, etc.
- ☐ other pastors or Christian workers, as a supervisor, coordinator, regional director, consultant, or director of an organization
- ☐ This depends on further information.

If you will work with a *small group* (part of a larger church) mark how:
- ☐ as supervisor of several small groups
- ☐ as a small group leader
- ☐ as an active member of a small group
- ☐ This depends on further information.

If your primary ministry is to mobilize your church as a *missionary sending base*, mark what the missionaries will do:
- ☐ start daughter churches nearby (perhaps among ethnic groups)
- ☐ start churches in distant fields (including among unreached people)
- ☐ reproduce small home churches or cells, for pastoral care and evangelism in their own community
- ☐ a combination of the above
- ☐ This depends on further information.

If *pastoral training* is your main ministry (preparing pastors/elders for shepherding ministry), where?
- ☐ with a church planting team locally or overseas.
- ☐ with a theological institution.
- ☐ in the churches, in a pioneer field.
- ☐ This depends on further information.

If your main ministry involves _long-range planning for church reproduction_, indicate how:

- ☐ as a pastor of a reproducing church
- ☐ as an executive with a mission agency
- ☐ as a church planter in a pioneer field
- ☐ as a teacher or curriculum writer
- ☐ as a mission-related career counselor
- ☐ This depends on further information.

3. Use this Guide to train others _in a church context._

If you use this guide with a mission agency or team that is not a church, you may need to form a _temporary_ church for training purposes. During the time you study together, you do many of the activities listed in this guide, in order to acquire the skills needed to multiply churches. Even if your group is very small, name temporary elders. Meet with them to plan worship together as a small group and celebrate Communion. This enables you to make plans and commitments as a body in which different spiritual gifts interact, rather than in a classroom, where only the gift of teaching is in operation. In years of teaching church multiplication skills, we have seen few acquire them outside a church. (If you hope to be the exception, good luck! You might also try to learn high diving in the classroom.)

The benefits of this church-based team training will become more apparent as you progress. Remember, simply _being_ an obedient church is as important as the goal itself. Not only will you learn the skills for growth and reproduction, but you will also begin the very process in which the cycle of reproduction continues--the church!

Cross-cultural church planters need to be _stretched_ in order to relate to other cultures, such as God stretched Peter in Acts 10 by telling him to eat unclean animals in a vision. Let this temporary church worship stretch you! It will help you see firsthand the problems faced by cross-cultural church planters.

Cross-cultural church planters also need experience with the essentials of worship and must distinguish them from their own culturally specific style of worship. Let this temporary church give you a chance to adapt worship to a small group, without electronic sound, skilled musicians, or a large sanctuary.

4. Develop _Activity Review Files._

To record your plans, we recommend the use of _Activity Review Files_ (ARFs). This guide itself serves as a manual for starting and developing churches, if you begin at once to apply relevant items to your ministry and organization. Please do not read it as you would read a regular book. Use it prayerfully to _list your activity plans_, for later use as a checklist as you move toward your long-range goals. We call this type of checklist an "Activity Review File" because it can also serve as a functional file system. To save time, you may simply mark items for now that you will list later in an ARF. Please remember to mark the box o in Appendix E _Items to Review_ for all items throughout this _Guide_ that apply to you or your disciples so you can incorporate them into your ministry and plans. Use Appendix E as a _check list_ to help prepare your ARFs.

You may also want to help those you lead, train, or serve to prepare an ARF for the people they will work with. For example, if they serve with a new church, help them to prepare an ARF with activities that the church members will do, led by their own leaders. This helps a church planting team made up of outsiders to phase out as it trains new local leaders.

If you already have an alphabetical, topical, or biblical file system, cross-reference relevant items in your ARFs. For example, make a note in your ARF under "Witnessing" about useful information on evangelism in your previous topical file. This enables you to relate the theory to the practice in a practical and systematic way.

An ARF enables you to:

1. _Record plans_ for yourself, your disciples, and your organization;
2. _Evaluate progress_ for yourself, your disciples, and your organization;
3. _File materials_ where they support a definite future activity;
4. _Build training curriculum_ around the church's activities (if you are a teacher). If you train leaders on the job, an ARF enables you to group material around church activities rather than around topics. This is explained fully in chapter 16 below.

If you already have a filing system that does these four things well, disregard the further information in this section about Activity Review Files. If you do not have such a system, please prepare an ARF with your coworkers. Start with a checklist of what you believe God wants you and your church(es) to do. But do not list the activities on one sheet of paper. Rather, list each major activity category as

the title (a verb) on a separate file folder. Use this ARF with a helper (adviser, discipler, colleague, teammate, or teacher) to help you guide the ministry of your team or church.

You may need two or three ARFs--one for yourself, one for the new churches, and one for your church planting team. For example, as you gain insights about cross-cultural evangelism, note them under an activity on evangelism. Do not simply file these plans and insights in an alphabetical limbo, but put them under activities that you or your disciples will do in the future.

Examples of **Activity Review Files:**

For a **personal** ARF see *Appendix A.*

For a **new church** ARF, *Appendix B.*

For a **church planting team** ARF, *Appendix C.*

For a **sending church** ARF, *Appendix D.*

Again, we encourage you to use an ARF together with coworkers with whom you can discuss plans and evaluate them as you progress. An ARF is like the bark of dog, which may be a greeting but also a warning. As a checklist, it enables you to specify your plans in a way that will remind you what to do and then let you evaluate it once you have done it. Many great visions fail because they are not set down in a system that is easy to implement. Others fail because they are never ruthlessly evaluated and adjusted to changing situations. Many church programs begin in response to a need and are powerfully used by God for a time, only to continue as a hollow tradition absorbing valuable resources like a sponge when we lack the courage to evaluate them ruthlessly and make needed changes.

Richard Scoggins relates an example of how he learned the value of such ruthless evaluation:

The first church I was involved in planting basically came into existence and grew through neighborhood evangelistic Bible studies. After about four years,

however, no new believers were being added to the church through the Bible studies. They were still well attended--but by church members, not unbelievers! After trying to revive them for a year to fulfill their original intention, we concluded they could not be revived and so we ended them, which caused a huge uproar by the congregation. The valuable resources (the teachers), we concluded, could be better used in other areas. Make no mistake, if you desire to grow and reproduce, you will have to make many unpopular decisions, based on clear objectives and ruthless evaluations.

5. **Depending on your ministry, you may want to prepare more than one of the following types of** *Activity Review Files:*

   a. For *pastors/elders* who help their church to multiply. List the activities God wants your church to do; start with the obvious--the explicit commands of Jesus Christ--and build your ministry plans on this foundation of loving obedience. Then you will know that you are proceeding in God's will. (See Appendix D.)

   b. For *church planters* multiplying churches in a pioneer field.

   Start listing activities that the new churches will do, and file pertinent information under them. If you have not yet bonded with the people and culture, you will revise this ARF radically when you do so (see Appendix B.)

   c. For your own *personal ministry.*

   You may want to start a personal ARF now also, listing things you and your family will do, to reach your God-given, life goals (see Appendix A.)

   d. For a *church planting team.*

   You would list things that the team members--not the churches--would do, such as get acquainted with the people in a new area, learn the language, etc. (see Appendix C.)

Examples of ARFs with their activity titles and related study appear in Appendices A-D at the end of this guide. Please do not simply copy them; develop your own plans prayerfully, geared to the needs of your own church, field, and disciples. Keep revising and adapting these ARFs so that they guide you and your coworkers toward your goals. Keep gearing them to the circumstances, abilities, and objectives of those you work with.

When you add an activity category in an ARF, write its title as an *action verb* ("Witness," "Organize the Elders," "Baptize," etc.) on the tab of the file folder. Do not simply list the activities on a sheet of paper (this hinders revising and rearranging the activities later on). As you check the brackets by items in this guide that you plan to apply to your work, also list plans under the related ARF activities.

If you use more than one ARF, determine which one best relates to items you mark in this guide. For example, if the bracket you check concerns something you do yourself, list plans or information about it in a personal ARF. If the item is something for workers in the new churches, list it in an ARF for the new churches' leaders (normally prepared by the pastoral trainer on the church planting team). If the bracket checked involves an item for the church planting team, list it in a team ARF (normally prepared by the team leader). If the item concerns an established church, list it in an ARF containing activities that the congregation or small groups will do.

Add new ARF activities as your plans take shape. To monitor and guide your progress, keep revising and adapting the ARF with an adviser or colleague with whom you discuss your work as you move toward your goals. If you still find it hard to visualize an Activity Review File, don't be too concerned now. It will become clearer as you work through this guide.

6. Suggested Reading

Some items in this guide recommend *Bible studies*. Get God's view first of each principle of church reproduction, before you read other Books about it, in order to resist traditions that might stifle it. Study these passages with your colleagues if a principle is new to you. For further reading on church multiplication, we recommend:

Training materials (several booklets and a general manual) by Richard Scoggins. Available from the *Fellowship of Church Planters*, 75 Capron Farm Drive, Warwick, RI 02886.

Obedience Oriented Education, George Patterson. Principles of church reproduction through discipling, from the viewpoint of an educator of pastors; available from Church Planting International, 9521-A Business Center Drive, Cucamonga, CA 91730.

Perspectives on the World Christian Movement, edited by Ralph Winter and Steven Hawthorne (Pasadena: William Carey Library, 1981). See the articles in the section on strategy. Available from William Carey Bookstore, 1605 Elizabeth, Pasadena, CA 91104.

Church Planting Workbook (for use in the U.S.), Robert Logan and Jeff Rast. 1985. Fuller Evangelistic Institute, P.O. Box 91990, Pasadena, CA 91109.

7. **Implementation: As you read through this *Guide*, record the numbered items in Appendix E *Items to Review* that you plan to discuss with your co-workers. Also, write here now in a general way how you will record your plans in your ARFs:**

_____

_____

_____

_____

_____

_____

_____

_____

_____

_____

_____

_____

_____

_____

_____

Remember: mark items by number in Appendix E *Items to Review* , to deal with later, or to plan together with your co-workers.

Key Terms Defined, as Used in this Book:

Apostle: *A cross-cultural church planter, sent to a new area.* The word "apostle" has two meanings in the New Testament: as a title referring to the Twelve whom Jesus chose to accompany Him, and also merely as a "sent one." We use the word in the second sense, as Luke did to refer to Barnabas and others who were not among the original Twelve. In an apostolic ministry we should imitate the apostles (especially Paul), who:
- ✔ were sent by God as career, cross-cultural church planters,
- ✔ worked as a team, often in fields closed to open missionary activity, multiplying small house churches,
- ✔ sometimes had secular employment of a type that kept them close to the common people,
- ✔ often had their message confirmed by healing or signs.

Church: *A group of believers of any size, committed to one another and to obeying Jesus' commands.* Our Lord in his Great Commission commands us with "all authority in heaven and earth" to disciple all peoples by teaching them to obey all his commands; these include celebrating the Lord's Supper and other activities that are done only by a body (a church).

Church growth: *Conversion of sinners to Jesus Christ--that is, salvation through outreach.* This guide does not deal with "biological" or "transfer" growth.

Church planter: *One who helps starts a church* anywhere.

Church reproduction or **multiplication**: *The voluntary multiplication of a church of any size, by God's power, in daughter churches or cells that in turn plant granddaughters, and so forth.* We refer to *church* reproduction because it is an obedient congregation rather than individual members that reproduces as the living, reproducing body of the Son of God. An obedient church, in which our God-given gifts are harmonized in love by the power of the Holy Spirit, has an inherent, God-given power to multiply itself indefinitely, just as all other living things do that God has created. Growth by *addition* is seen in Acts 2:41, when 3,000 converts were added by baptism to the new church in Jerusalem. Growth by *multiplication* appears in Acts 8, 10, 13, 14, and 16, where daughter churches are born. Church reproduction also refers to small groups or cells within a church, if they provide total pastoral care and true discipling.

Corporate disciple: *One who responds to Jesus' call to follow him as part of his body the church and who unites with a body of believers with the same corporate mentality.* God calls believers into a special relationship with other subjects in his kingdom. Corporate disciples consider themselves to be called to build the church in loving cooperation with others (Col. 1:24-29). As we grow in obedience, change occurs in our actions and attitudes toward others. In a discipling church these motivations for our behavior are exposed and developed in the

power of the Holy Spirit. As healing occurs, a corporate disciple is freed for more effective service (Gal. 5:13). In corporate discipling we consciously make disciples who are added to the body and its corporate life. Normally it starts with baptism. One covenants with other believers to obey Jesus Christ and his apostles as a body. Then he becomes active in ministry and is voluntarily accountable to a loving discipler (John 13:34; Acts 2:41-37; Matt. 28:18-20; Heb. 13:17) rather than in legalistic submission to a dictatorial discipler.

Elder: *A copastor serving with other elders, authorized by his church to shepherd.* Normally, elders help oversee the work, coordinating the use of the differing gifts in the body. No one elder or pastor does *everything*. One may oversee the Lord's Supper and baptisms, although he delegates these responsibilities to responsible brothers who work under his oversight. Another may oversee congregational meetings by delegating this responsibility to others who take turns. A reproducing church has elders who constantly reproduce themselves in all that they do, so that members of the congregation are continually equipped to teach, counsel, run congregational meetings, lead small group meetings, disciple, etc. Jesus spent most of his public ministry time equipping his disciples to carry on church reproduction after he left; elders should do the same (Eph. 4:12-13).

Evangelist: *One whose main ministry is witnessing for Jesus Christ in private or public and bringing the converts into fellowship with the body.*

House church: *A congregation meeting in homes, small offices, or rented facilities to assure continued growth through multiplication by avoiding limitations imposed by ever-expanding facilities or centralized control.* The clusters of house churches to which the authors refer maintain loving, cooperative fellowship with churches that meet in larger facilities, and practice obedient, corporate discipleship (in contrast to certain earlier house church movements characterized by divisively independent, legalistic leadership).

Leaders: *"Leaders" will be considered to be elders in the biblical sense, unless otherwise specified.* This Guide assumes that the primary goal of leadership is to equip the saints and coordinate the efforts of the members of the body for its edification (including its reproduction). Leaders who simply control rather than help others to minister are a major reason why churches fail to reproduce.

Pioneer field: *A people group with no churches yet* which disciple their own people within their own culture.

Small group: *A home group or cell that does pastoral care, evangelism and perhaps other ministries* (not *just* Bible study or fellowship).

PART 1 - Church Multiplication Arising from Obeying Jesus' Commands

"Don't listen to any voice that tells you that your organization's policies (or anything else) comes first!"

1. The Need for Total, Childlike Obedience

Recommended Bible Study: Acts 2:36-47. You might relate this reading as a story, for adults and young people alike. **First**, ask the people you are studying with to look for what the converts did in obedience to Jesus in order to be baptized and received into the church. Look also for what they did in obedience to Jesus immediately after their baptism. **Second**, look in Matthew 28:16-20 for why we should obey Jesus. Discuss what Jesus' authority is. See also John 14:15 (discuss what our motivation should be) and John 15:1-17 (discuss what Jesus does for us now).

8. Commit yourself to *obey Jesus' specific commands* before and above all else.

This guide explains many factors in church multiplication, but the one most significant factor--way out ahead of anything else--is simply obeying the Lord Jesus Christ above all else, in childlike faith and love.

Don't listen to any voice that tells you that your organization's policies (or anything else) comes first! Above all else, church multiplication comes through *teaching obedience to Christ*. We build our plans, activities, and commitments for church reproduction on Jesus' commands--the specific things he emphasized over and over in many ways and contexts, the things that his disciples must do. They can be summarized in seven general categories, or basic commands. If you do not already know them, you *must* memorize them, because they are the basic building blocks for discipling and church planting:

1. **Repent, believe, and receive the Holy Spirit**
2. **Be baptized**
3. **Love God and neighbor**
4. **Break bread**
5. **Pray**
6. **Give**
7. **Disciple others**

We include the apostles' commands in the New Testament with Jesus' commands, as they were given to us in Scripture with the inspired authority of Christ. Their commands in the Epistles, however, are for leaders and more mature Christians, who are already baptized and under the care of a church.

We might learn better to focus on direct, childlike obedience from the experience of others. George Patterson relates:

I discovered the value of simple, direct, childlike obedience to Jesus' commands during a time of painful controversy. While multiplying churches in Honduras, our more traditional pastors and missionaries found us too radical. We were letting the work grow beyond their control, and they criticized us vigorously. (If you plan for God to use you as an instrument to multiply churches, be prepared for similar trials.) I felt insecure. Were we doing God's will? Who was to say what was right or wrong? It seemed at the time that so many of our Christian brothers were against us. They followed whoever shouted the loudest, or was higher in the organization. I tried shouting, too, but it didn't work for me. I had no title or authority. I was simply a discipler of voluntary, lay pastoral trainees in an informal extension program. Confused and bruised, we called our discouraged trainees together to pray and told them, "From now on, we will base *everything* on the commands of Jesus for his disciples." We memorized the commands of Christ and agreed, whenever anyone criticized, to tell them, "We are obeying Jesus' commands and imitating his apostles. Would you rather we obeyed and imitated you?"

God blessed this commitment. Even though criticism continued, we felt liberated. We were on solid ground. Let the critics say what they may! We were obeying Jesus because he is the divine Head of the church (Col. 1:15-20). We obeyed him because we loved him for what he was doing for us. He said, "If you love me, obey my commands" (John 14:15).

Let us consider Jesus' claim on our obedience. During his incarnation on earth, he did so many miracles and good works that people were whispering that he was the promised Christ (Messiah). Some even said he was the Son of God. So the Judean supreme court tried him for blasphemy. The high priest asked him, "Are you the Son of the Blessed?" Everything hung on Jesus' answer--which was a clear "Yes!" That ended the trial. The high priest tore his robes in fury, and immediately the council condemned Jesus to death. This made his resurrection doubly important, for besides the fact of his new life was the proof that he was who he said. Shortly after, on the basis of his proven deity, the risen Jesus commanded his followers, "All authority is given to me. . . . Therefore make disciples of all nations . . . teaching them to obey all that I have commanded" (Matt. 28:18-20).

Discipling the nations is *obedience training*. True church planting and pastoral work normally stems from loving obedience to the commands of him who has "all authority in heaven and earth." The apostles, for example, started the first church in Jerusalem while their Lord's Great Commission was still ringing in their ears: "Disciple all peoples . . . teaching them to obey all my commands." When the Holy Spirit came and enabled them to start putting this into practice, they did exactly what Jesus said to do (Acts 2). They started discipling a people (their own Jewish nation), instructing them to obey all his commands.

By the end of the chapter we find 3,000 converts who obey all of Jesus' basic commands: they repent, believe, and receive the Holy Spirit; they are baptized; they celebrate the Lord's Supper; they love God and one another in fervent fellowship; they pray, give, and devote themselves to the apostles' teaching; and they witness to others--everything Jesus specifically ordered them to do. If you have pastoral experience, you know that this did not happen by accident. The apostles consciously trained them to obey Jesus' commands.

The ensuing activities in the book of Acts, as well as the doctrines, commands, and ministries in the Epistles, grow out of these basic commands of our risen Lord and the historical events that were called "the gospel"--that is, the good news of Jesus' death and resurrection. Good pastoral ministries build upon these basic commands and truths. For example, Paul's command to Titus to establish elders (Titus 1:5) is an extension (in this case, to Crete) of Jesus' original command to disciple all nations. The apostle Paul delegates this discipling to his disciple Titus who, in turn, delegates it to the new elders in Crete. Throughout the letter Paul gives Titus detailed instructions on mobilizing the elders. No totally new commands are found in the Epistles; everything commanded by the apostles builds on Jesus' original commands or applies them to specific situations. Only this loving, faithful obedience to the divine Head of the church--nothing else taking precedence--allows normal growth and reproduction of churches.

Describe your personal commitment to obey Jesus:

_____

_____

_____

_____

_____

_____

_____

_____

9. Make disciples who before all else *obey Jesus' basic commands.*

For adults newly converted in a pioneer field, this obedience normally starts with baptism (Matt. 28:18-20; Acts 2:36-42). Baptism has a vertical as well as a horizontal dimension: converts display their commitment to God and also become identified with fellow believers (Acts 2:41-47). Thus baptism of an adult convert can be an effective initiation into corporate discipleship. The basic commands of Jesus have a horizontal as well as a vertical purpose. A hermit can in no way carry out the commands of Christ. A heavy emphasis on doctrinal teaching without the corresponding application of love--a common imbalance in the Western church--feeds on the radical individualism produced by Renaissance philosophy, not Kingdom theology. Nothing takes precedence over loving, faithful, childlike obedience to our loving Lord.

Without an orientation to obedience to the basic commands of their Lord, Christian workers follow church traditions, rules, and human scruples, which stifle spontaneous church growth and reproduction. Especially in a pioneer field where they lack the model of a well-organized church and experienced pastors/elders, new leaders will overemphasize nonessentials: they will seek subsidies and will control God's people with nonbiblical rules for ordination, baptism, marriage, evangelism methods, church planting procedures, and pastoral training methods. Church planters who are not orientated to obedience use traditional evangelism methods that rarely result directly in obedient, corporate disciples. They inevitably overprotect their new churches, because they cannot trust converts who have not learned to obey Jesus.

As you train your converts in a pioneer field to do these things, overcoming the barriers to love by continued repentance and renewing of the mind according to the Word, you will have a church that can reproduce! It will not be easy, and of course you first must learn how to overcome the barriers to love in your own life. But if you keep to the basics and continue to lean on and learn from the Lord, you can start a network of reproducing churches that will "infect" this world for the Lord Jesus!

Church reproduction in the power of the Spirit of God is linked with starting and developing churches whose activities are based squarely on the basic commands of Jesus, doing just as he orders us to do. We consciously follow the example of his apostles, starting with their model of discipling in Acts 2.

We endanger the spiritual life of Christians if we teach them a lot of heavy, detailed Bible facts and doctrine before they learn basic obedience in love. The Holy Spirit's power to transform the converts in Acts 2 is seen in their immediate, loving obedience. To make corporate disciples in a truly biblical way, we teach obedience to these basic commands before all else. We obey our divine Head immediately, without argument or discussion. Baptism, for example, as commanded by Jesus and practiced by his apostles, came immediately after conversion; it was not a graduation ceremony following a long time of indoctrination and probation (Matt. 28:18-20; Acts 2:41; 8:12, 36-38; 10:44-48; 16:14-15, 29-34; 18:8; 22:12-16).

We do not vote on whether or not we obey these commands. A vote puts the authority of the majority over Almighty God. His church is not a democracy but a monarchy--a kingdom. We obey Jesus' commands simply, directly, like a child, in *love*. To obey for other motives is legalism, which God condemns (see Rom. 13:8-10; 1 Cor. 13:1-3). Jesus summarized the Old Testament com-

---

Jesus' commands can be described further, as follows:

1. **Repent, believe, and receive the Holy Spirit**. These go together; we cannot do one without the others (Mark 1:15; John 20:22).

2. **Be baptized**. This command includes living forever the new, holy life it signifies (Matt. 28:19-20; see also Rom. 6:1-4).

3. **Love** God, family, fellow disciples, neighbor, and even enemies. This command thus teaches forgiveness (Luke 10:25-37; Matt. 6:44).

4. **Celebrate the Lord's Supper**. This includes cultivating the communion with Christ and his people that the Eucharist affirms (Matt. 26:26-28).

5. **Pray** daily (Matt. 6:5-13; Luke 11:9).

6. **Give** generously (Matt. 6:19-21; Luke 6:38).

7. **Make disciples**. This includes evangelism, teaching obedience, shepherding, and training pastors (Matt. 28:18-19; Luke 24:46-48; see also 2 Tim. 2:2).

mands of God (including the Ten Commandments) in two laws: love God; love your neighbor. Healthy church reproduction requires that we make disciples who, above all else, lovingly obey the basic commands of him who has all authority in heaven and on earth (Matt. 28:18-20; John 14:15). As disciples are taught to obey the basic commands of our Lord and begin to do so, barriers to obedience will become evident in their attitudes and feelings. As these are honestly faced, confessed, and repented of, the obedience of the disciples will lead to progressively deeper love for God and their neighbors. As we increasingly practice corporate discipleship, we will be better able to see this lack of love, which will be more evident toward our visible brothers than toward our invisible God, even though the two are inextricably connected (Matt. 25:31-46).

10. *Measure growth* in Christ by each person's obedience to him, in order to disciple as he commands.

To evaluate growth, especially in a new church in a pioneer field, we use two yardsticks. **First**, we measure progress in *obeying the commands of Jesus*, beginning with baptism of repentant converts (don't count unbaptized converts; see Rom. 6; Heb. 5:11-6:12). **Second**, this obedience normally leads to ministry (truly edifying church ministries grow out of at least one of Jesus' basic commands); thus we also measure progress in *mobilizing more mature members for ministry* as they use their spiritual gifts in loving harmony, edifying each other (see Eph. 4:1-16).

A healthy, obedient body that harmonizes its different spiritual gifts readily reproduces in daughter churches; trust God to give you people with the apostolic gift who will enable your church to reproduce relatively painlessly. They will probably also have other gifts (a church planting team needs a leader, evangelists, pastoral trainer, etc.).

11. *Discern human policies* as temporary and of secondary importance, to avoid rules or policies that stifle church multiplication.

Three assumptions often breed policies that impede normal church reproduction: first, the myth that it is somehow spiritual to delay obedience, often needlessly ("But we need a strong home base first!"); second, the assumption that we must use all available resources on that part of the church over which we have control ("We lack funds to meet our own needs, let alone those of a new church!"); finally, the fear that love for Christ and biblical truth will gradually diminish in a chain of new churches (daughter church, granddaughters, great-granddaughters, etc.).

The fear mentioned above is understandable; the new churches must remain doctrinally sound and loyal to Christ. But we often overlook the real source of sound doctrine and loyalty: *neither come from human control.* So sometimes we aim unwisely for the multiplication to extend from our own church like spokes extending from one hub (with no granddaughter churches, just daughters, as in the diagram below) so that we can control the work. This fear is often based on the assumption that our church must somehow be superior to other churches in the chain, that the Holy Spirit will be given to newer churches in a lesser measure! We must not forget that each new grain of corn engenders an entirely new plant with the same potential as its parent for healthy reproduction.

The above objections overlook the reason for the church's existence, which is both to be and to make obedient, sacrificial disciples, according to Jesus' mandate. This takes precedence over other policies and organizational plans. Of course, human rules and policies are needed to maintain order. So our commitment to obedience embraces a policy of temporary rules. Our own man-made rules for a truly obedient church are temporary, for a given need. We should erase them as soon as the need is dealt with, or else they become permanent traditions—sacred cows that stand in the way of obedience to Christ first and the freedom that stems from it.

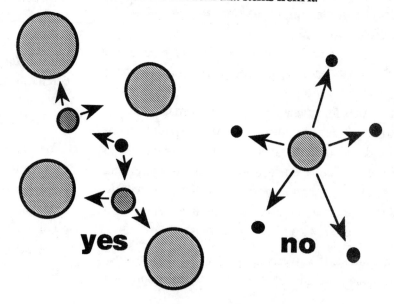

yes   no

12. For discipling that reproduces, help members learn to discern Jesus' commands.

<u>Recommended Bible Study: Matt. 15:1-20</u>. Find how Jesus treated traditions that hinder obedience.

For effective reproductive discipling, we discern the levels of authority for church activities. We find three such levels:

1. **New Testament commands,**
2. **Apostolic practices** (not commanded),
3. **Human traditions** (customs).

To establish our authority for discipling, we teach our people to discern clearly between New Testament commands (which form the basis for discipling), mere apostolic practices (not commanded), and human traditions. Most church divisions are caused by power-hungry leaders who take some mere apostolic practice (which was not commanded) or human tradition and make it a law, placing it on the same level as the commands of Christ. Many churches have been divided or discouraged by nonbiblical rules for worship methods, dress codes, church procedures, membership or baptism requirements, ordination or pastoral training requirements, policies, bylaws, and so forth. There can be no spontaneous, loving obedience to Jesus as long as his authority is confused with man-made rules.

Here are examples of *apostolic practices* that were not commanded to be done by everybody:

✔ Laying on of hands to receive the Holy Spirit or to commission workers;

✔ Fasting;

✔ Speaking in tongues and the exercise of other spiritual gifts;

✔ Sharing material goods in common;

✔ Using one cup for the Lord's Supper;

✔ Celebrating the Lord's Supper in homes each Sunday, or more frequently;

✔ Baptizing immediately.

We cannot demand these things; only Christ has the authority to command things for his church. Since the apostles practiced them, we cannot prohibit them. A church certainly has the liberty to imitate the apostles when circumstances are favorable.

Here are several examples of *evangelical traditions* not

---

3 *LEVELS*
OF AUTHORITY FOR CHRISTIANS

1. New Testament commands. Christ requires obedience to his commands by his disciples; we practice them under all circumstances; we never prohibit them (examples: repent, believe, recieve the Spirit, be baptized, love, break bread, pray, give, make disciples, forgive, love our wives, obey our spiritual elders, name elders in the churches, discipline unruly members, witness for Christ, etc.).

2. Apostolic practices (not commanded). We do not have the authority to require or to prohibit the practice of the things that the apostles did but that God himself neither commanded nor prohibited. Only Christ the Head of the church has this kind of authority over his body.

3. Human customs (no mention in the New Testament). The only authority of a human tradition lies in our voluntary agreement with a local congregation, which God recognizes as binding (see Matt. 18:18-20). We cannot force them on other congregations; we prohibit them when they impede obedience.

---

mentioned in Scripture. They are not necessarily *wrong;* they are merely traditions that, in some circumstances have been blessed by God and in other cases have hindered discipling:

✔ Sunday School; Christian education programs that segregate young people by age;

✔ Pulpits, loudspeakers, pianos, organs, televised worship, the public invitation to raise hands or walk forward to "accept Christ";

✔ Using baptism as a graduation ceremony following a prolonged period of probation or indoctrination;

✔ Equating correctional discipline with specific periods of time of exclusion from fellowship or communion;

✔ Making a lecture-type sermon the center and climax of worship (instead of the Lord's Supper);

✔ Isolating the gift of teaching, making it an end in

itself by preparing leaders outside of the body in which different gifts are exercised in harmony;

✔ Professional, paid church staffs;

✔ Institutional mission agencies;

✔ Nonbiblical ordination requirements.

Human customs receive lowest priority in our plans; we never demand them; we permit them if they edify and are agreed upon in love. We forbid them, of course, when they impede direct obedience to Jesus. They are most dangerous when they become institutionalized, with money, organizational power, or legality behind them.

Evangelical policies that commonly impede the spontaneous reproduction of churches in pioneer fields include *nonbiblical rules* for:

✔ naming and training new pastors or elders;

✔ officiating at the Lord's Supper, baptism, and marriage;

✔ organizing new churches;

✔ control from the outside (often with foreign funds).

13. **Implementation:** Add your detailed plans now to your *Activity Review Files* (together with your co-workers, if possible); list plans under the corresponding ministry activities. Also, please write your general, overall plan *now* for your people to obey the basic commands of Christ in simple, childlike faith and love:

_____

_____

_____

_____

_____

_____

_____

_____

_____

_____

Did you forget to mark items in the last Appendix that you want to review later?

That's OK. Why bother?

Let others make the sacrifice to multiply churches!

2. Obeying Jesus' Command to Repent, Believe, and Receive the Holy Spirit

<u>**Recommended Bible Story: Luke 24**</u>. Look for the importance of the resurrection as a basic part of the gospel story; look also for the bare, essential truths of the gospel message in verses 45-49 (compare John 20:22 and Acts 1:8).

14. Do simply what Jesus commands to do to be saved--repent and believe.

Perhaps you have heard it whispered, that all you have to do to be saved is to make a *decision*. To repent, as Jesus made plain, is not simply to make a decision. This is Western thinking. Repentance is *turning from evil to serve God*. On the negative side, we die with Jesus to sin; on the positive side, we participate in his new, pure resurrection life by faith. To achieve merely the negative side even to sinless perfection brings us up only to the level of a neutral object or irrational animal (a rock or a toad is sinless); one still lacks loving obedience.

George Patterson relates how God revealed the error of exporting Western decision-making methods to another culture:

Several times in Central America we participated in evangelistic campaigns, both mass meetings and personal evangelism, that used methods developed in another culture (usually the U.S.). We found that it was easy to get decisions but that follow-through was nil. In that culture we could not multiply churches tied to such evangelism methods. So we had to rethink what conversion really is. We had a meeting with our workers and asked them not to report again as converts those who had simply made a decision or raised their hand to accept Jesus. (Is there something wrong with him that we have to accept him?) Such decisions were not valid in that culture: less than one in a hundred followed through. We prayed and asked the workers to aim simply at repentance and faith in Jesus as they evangelized.

They were doubtful at first; killing their sacred cow was painful. With Bibles open, we helped them to think it through: to be saved from our sins, all persons are commanded by our Lord to repent, believe, and receive the Holy Spirit (Mark 1:15; John 20:22). We group these three things together because we cannot do one without the other two. To repent and believe means we turn from sin and obey our risen Savior Jesus in childlike faith. This requires the help of the Spirit of God within us. There is no other way to be saved from the consequences of our sin, which is eternal judgment (Acts 4:12; Rev. 20:11-15).

Richard Scoggins also found a similar problem with "decisions" in a more-educated society:

We have found in Rhode Island that evangelism that seeks a decision is often destructive when measured against a gospel that seeks to invite people to join Christ in his Kingdom. Often people have made a profession of faith, but their life is left untouched by God's Spirit. They evidence none of the power of the Spirit in their life, which enables them to love God and their neighbor. In most such cases we have found that such persons are indeed unsaved but think they are saved! We are reminded that Satan is a master of deception; he has marked the road to hell with signs that read, "Heaven--this way." It is sad to see so many who have professed belief in Christ deny him by their life. Such persons will awaken to a tragically surprising eternity (Matt. 7:13-27).

We encourage our church planters and leaders not to count someone as in the Kingdom (i.e., as a convert) until that one has followed the pattern of the first converts in Acts 2: repent, be baptized, and be added to the believing congregation.

An essential pastoral ministry corresponding to Jesus' command to repent and believe (as well as to make disciples) is that of mobilizing our people to be his witnesses (Acts 1:8). Immediately after receiving the Holy Spirit on the Day of Pentecost, the apostles began witnessing for Jesus with power, calling the people of Jerusalem to repentance and faith (Acts 2). Obedient missionaries and their disciples will witness in a way that brings repentance and faith to those who have not received the Good News. Before all else, converts must appreciate the value of Jesus' death and resurrection for them and their families (Luke 24:44-48; John 4:35).

15. Witness as the apostles did, to bring about faith and repentance.

What kind of message brought faith and repentance in the power of the Spirit in the apostolic church? As Jesus commanded in Luke 24:44-48, the apostle Peter emphasized the following truths as he witnessed in Acts 2:

✔ **Who Jesus *is***: a man accredited by God by miracles, Lord and Messiah (Acts 2:22-36);

✔ **The value of his *death* for us**: forgiveness (Acts 2:23, 38);

✔ **The value of his *resurrection* for us**: victory, life through God's Holy Spirit, salvation (Acts 2:24-36, 38-40);

✔ **Our *response***: repentance, faith in Jesus, baptism, being added to a community of believers (Acts 2:38-41).

16. Implementation:

If you have not marked the numbered items that you intend to work on later, in Appendix E *Items to Review*, do so while they are fresh in your mind. With your co-workers, add these plans and commitments in the form of small, easy-to-take steps, in your ARFs, under activities on witnessing, believing and repenting. Also, please write *now* your general plan or commitment in response to Jesus' command to repent, believe and receive the Holy Spirit:

_____

_____

_____

_____

_____

_____

_____

_____

_____

_____

_____

_____

_____

_____

_____

_____

_____

_____

_____

_____

_____

3. Obeying Jesus' Command to Baptize

Recommended Bible Stories: Matthew 3 and Acts 8:26-40. Look in Acts 8:26-40 for who was baptized, when, and by whom.

17. For converts to be born from the very beginning as obedient disciples, *confirm salvation with baptism* without delay.

Inexperienced pastors often delay baptism out of caution. If safety is our concern, however, let us rather be more concerned that new believers obey Jesus above anything else. Scoggins speaks out of his experience with new churches:

New leaders often worry too much that tares will be admitted with the wheat. We teach them from the beginning that Satan is excellent at making counterfeits. Our highest barriers to baptism and addition to the church will not keep out his counterfeits. Instead of requiring extended probation, the church needs to learn and practice church discipline (Matt. 18:15-20). God himself did the first act of church discipline (Acts 5:1-11). Jesus taught, and Paul reinforced the idea, that the church itself is to take responsibility for maintaining purity (1 Cor. 5:1-13). We find that "low" barriers to being baptized and added to the church cause no problem as long as the church disciplines. But by delaying baptism and therefore neglecting church discipline, we make converts doubly disobedient! These are unpopular decisions for those who develop reproducing churches in a tolerant, rebellious world.

Patterson also relates:

In our early ministry in Honduras, we caused a sharp conflict because we baptized "too soon," according to some pastors. We missionaries had unwittingly taught the new pastors to be *too careful* whom they baptized. It came to be considered spiritual to delay baptism until all aspects of a convert's life were in order. But when we began discipling the same way that Jesus and the apostles did, this extreme carefulness had to be set aside. Our newer workers became "careless" with the grace of

Don't baptize that guy so soon!

He might fall !

God: they let it slop over on the unworthy! We observed the results with great interest. This "sloppiness" enabled the less careful pastors to bring nearly all of their converts to maturity and obedience. At the same time, nearly all of the more "careful" pastors' converts fell back into their former life without Christ. These "careful" pastors criticized us saying, "Oh, anyone can fill their churches if they baptize just anyone like you do, if you don't straighten out their lives first."

As the criticism grew intense we again felt insecure. Our converts were obviously growing and obeying Jesus to a much greater degree than the converts in the legalistic churches. But that only prodded our more legalistic brothers to seek more and more things to complain about in our way of working. It became obvious that nothing would satisfy them, short of turning control of our discipling program over to them. They would have ended it. Most painful was the fact that these criticisms came from our brothers in Christ whom we loved and respected.

So . . . more meetings! We helped our workers discover about baptism prayerfully in the Bible: that the apostles from the very beginning helped repentant converts to obey the commands of Jesus, starting with baptism--immediately. Seeing that the 3,000 converts in Acts 2:36-47 were baptized the same day they received Jesus in their hearts, we knew we had God's permission to do away with the many man-made rules of things to do before baptism. (These rules involved good things; the problem was that they became requirements for baptism--the initial confirmation of salvation--and canceled out the grace of God.) Our converts, like those in ancient Jerusalem, started at once to obey Jesus before receiving detailed doctrinal study (which came soon after).

Jesus instituted baptism to confirm the convert's salvation. Especially in another culture, we do not introduce man-made decision rites from our own culture to confirm salvation. The invitation of the apostles, for example, was not to raise one's hand or to "come forward," nor any other similar sacrament of non-biblical origin. Rather, their call was simply to be baptized (Acts 2:41).

If a church confirms one's salvation without rebaptizing a convert who was baptized as an infant, it must provide a meaningful ceremony if the traditional confirmation teaching and ceremony has become mechanical. This ceremony for new believers should include a happy celebration--a blessing bestowed by God through the church.

The church planting team that went with Peter to Caesarea baptized converts without delay (Acts 10:44-48). They did not follow the modern tradition of making baptism into a graduation ceremony after a time of indoctrination and investigation. This passage shows that Peter considered that it would have been disobedience to God to delay baptism once he and his companions saw that Cornelius and his people had been converted by the Holy Spirit.

18. Help converts to trust the Holy Spirit to unite them invisibly to Jesus and to enable them to sense Jesus' continued presence, *through their baptism.*

Baptism in the Bible is much more than the moment of the ritual with water. It includes the continued, eternally new life in the risen Lord Jesus Christ (Rom. 6:1-11). Caring pastors immediately assure converts who are being baptized with water of the Holy Spirit's corresponding spiritual baptism, sealing, and sanctifying.

Scoggins emphasizes the corporate aspect of baptism:

In some cultures baptism and being added to the church are synonymous. We have found in America, however, that teaching about baptism sometimes involves only the *vertical* component--showing only that a person has decided to follow Jesus. Teaching on baptism should also include the *horizontal* component: being baptized into Jesus' body means a person also has been called into the service and fellowship of his church (1 Cor. 12:12-13). Since it sometimes takes a while in the radically individualistic West for new disciples to appreciate this horizontal dimension, we find it helpful to baptize them while they are still learning the meaning of the corporate salvation to which they have been called.

Once the new disciples realize the nature of their corporate calling, we encourage them to covenant with the church. This is usually confirmed symbolically at a meeting where hands are laid on the disciples after they affirm their desire to follow the Lord in the service and fellowship of the church. Thus, what was originally a one-step process (in Acts baptism clearly had both vertical and horizontal components) we have allowed to occur in a two-step process (being baptized and being added to the church). Ideally, these two things will still occur at the same time, but often they do not. We try to get them to occur as closely as possible, believing that both are essential steps of obedience.

A church planting team with an organization that is not a church and does not itself baptize, must organize a church that is organizationally separate from the parent body, in order to baptize and serve as the first "mother" church in a new field.

19. **Implementation:** Mark items that apply in Appendix E. Also, please note below your general plans in response to Jesus' command to baptize; later, with your co-workers, add them to your ARFs:

_____

_____

_____

_____

_____

_____

_____

_____

4. Obeying Jesus' Command to Make Disciples

Recommended Bible Study: Matthew 28:18-20; John 15:1-10. Look for the relationship between Jesus' authority, our love for him, and obedience.

Several pastoral ministries grow out of this general command to make disciples, such as:

- ✔ evangelism;
- ✔ nurturing new believers;
- ✔ cultivating the spiritual life of the believers;
- ✔ teaching the Word and biblical doctrine;
- ✔ pastoral care and counseling;
- ✔ foreign mission work;
- ✔ pastoral training;
- ✔ children's ministries;
- ✔ shepherding in general.

20. Teach new believers immediately the full meaning of *discipleship*.

Jesus commands us to hold to his teaching and to disciple others (John 8:31; Matt. 28:18-20). The new disciples in the original church in Jerusalem devoted themselves to the apostles' teaching from the beginning; it started right after their initial step of baptism (Acts 2:41-42). As mentioned above, baptism had the effect in the early church of identifying the believer with Christ as well as with his church. It emphasized immediately the importance of the disciples' accountability within the assembly to live a life of obedience. We teach a new believer at once that the church that God is bringing him into is like a family where we get to know each other intimately. Our lives are lived out in

the assembly so that barriers to the Spirit-filled life can be manifested and repentance and renewal can take place.

21. To assure continued reproduction, help converts who are still outside the church to become *obedient, corporate disciples*.

If we merely help converts to "decide" to "accept" Jesus--a concept foreign to the New Testament--we will have few committed disciples. Jesus told his disciples, "Follow me, and I will make you fishers of men" (Matt. 4:19). Discipling, from a biblical perspective, normally starts with witnessing to pre-Christians. One becomes a corporate disciple by responding to the gospel and being added to the church through repentance, faith, and baptism (Acts 2:38-41). Then, as discipling continues, the new Christian learns to obey the other commands of Christ and to serve in a ministry. We build everything on loving obedience.

22. Relate the Word to life and ministry, just as Jesus and his apostles modeled in their teaching.

As portrayed in Scripture, Bible teaching is intensely practical. We teach to build up the body of Christ, not just to impart knowledge. Such teaching consistently applies God's Word to one's hearers' lives and ministries (see 2 Tim. 3:14-17; note the purpose of all biblical instruction: to equip for ministry). Teaching in the church, done as the Word commands, has the specific objective of mobilizing church members for ministry (Eph. 4:11-16). The gift of

Discipling isn't no big deal. It's just to help new believers take off and fly straight.

That's not exactly what Jesus said.

teaching, as commanded by Scripture, is to be exercised strictly in harmony with the other gifts given to the body (1 Cor. 12).

23. To assure continued church reproduction, *disciple on all levels* of Christian maturity.

In time, we should be discipling on at least four levels:

1. The *unsaved*: the "nations" whom we disciple (Matt. 28:19);
2. *New Christians*: the converts whom we baptize and teach obedience (Matt. 28:19);
3. *Older Christians* (John 8:31; John 21:16);
4. *Top-level leaders*: pastors/elders or missionaries (Mark 3:13-19).

24. To mobilize men and women for ministry, *teach with loving authority.*

We teach with Jesus' authority, not our own or that of our organization. Our delegated authority is derived from Christ. We command with the Word of our Lord and of his inspired apostles (1 Tim. 4:11). Disciplers are weak if they depend on authority derived from a human hierarchy or organization ("You obey me because I have been named to this position over you!"). This authority depends on a loving, confidential relationship between the disciplers and each corporate disciple they train, especially those on the pastor/elder level. Unless it grows out of loving relationships, authoritative discipling stifles initiative. Good teachers take loving responsibility for their disciples' effective ministry; their disciples then eagerly follow their counsel and imitate their example.

Disciplers of pastors/elders train them far more effectively when they keep looking beyond the students to focus on the students' ministry in a church or group. Teachers actually build up the church through their students (Eph. 4:11-16; see the figure, right).

Our disciples do what we teach them, not because we are higher than they are in the organization (such church leadership is condemned by Jesus in Matt. 20:25-26), but because we love them and they have confidence in us. To mobilize new workers, we should work with corporate disciples with whom we can develop a loving relationship and who respect our God-given authority under Christ, as his undershepherds (Heb. 13:17).

25. To reproduce churches in a pioneer field, *integrate church planting with pastoral training.*

To illustrate this integration of church planting with pastoral training, Patterson recounts:

When we started using TEE (Theological Education by Extension) in Honduras, we followed the only model we knew. We merely opened more classrooms out in the villages, to make pastoral training available to those who could not leave their crops, families, jobs, or animals to come to our resident Bible Institute. This model had worked for the Presbyterians in Guatemala because they already had the churches and needed only to train their pastors. But we did not even have the churches. (There are no experienced pastors or well-established churches in pioneer fields.)

So our methods were failing. Those we trained, even by extension, were unable to raise up their own churches and pastor them. So . . . another meeting! The workers pleaded, "Not more changes!" But we explained the needed change: we could not multiply churches without shepherds (pastors/elders), or shepherds without churches. We raise up the two together. We started modeling it. We began on-the-job training for new leaders (elder types--not the single young men who had previously come to our resident Bible Institute). We helped them to grow along with their congregations. Churches began to multiply.

Again, the criti-

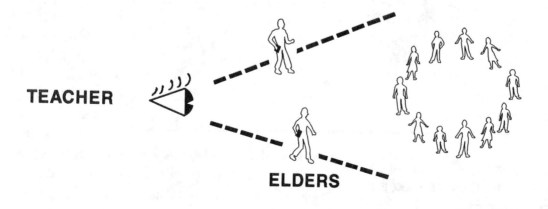

TEACHER

ELDERS

CHURCH

cisms. We were putting men into pastoral leadership too soon! Our national association of churches raised loud objections. In their national assembly they voted our discipling program out of existence. But we kept on existing. God continued to multiply churches. The leaders of the national association sent a harshly worded petition to the board of our mission agency demanding that I be removed from the field. We decided to pray it through rather than fighting the issue in the arenas of church and mission politics. The controversy fanned itself into a tornado.

We had more meetings to urge our workers, now officially disowned by our national level leaders, simply to keep obeying Jesus and close their ears to the criticisms. We told them, "Keep praying and applying the Word to the way we train and mobilize elders. Let us imitate the apostles; Paul named fairly new Christians as elders in Acts 14:23; there were no experienced elders available. We, like Paul and Barnabas, commission as elders the most mature men whom God provides. But out of respect to our critics, and to avoid further offense, we would call these new pastoral leaders 'provisional elders' because they are too new to be confirmed permanently in this pastoral role." In time the marriage became complete: church planting and pastoral training were united by God's Spirit in one combined program of church reproduction.

Every pioneer church planting team needs at least one gifted teacher who also has the gift of wisdom, as well as pastoral experience, to train new pastors/elders on the job. Other spiritual gifts helpful in integrating theory and practice as we train new pastors/elders may be those of teacher, prophet, or exhorter.

26. Help a convert teach the Word to his family.

Scoggins relates how he focuses on the family:

Usually in our churches we try to have the families prepare for the teaching times at our Sunday meetings. A Bible reading schedule is prepared by the leaders that can be used in the homes of those forming the community. Thus the heads of the home are taught from the beginning to take responsibility for shepherding in the home. This is often the first step in discovering and developing leaders, since leaders must be able to care for their own families. These reading schedules consist simply of a few assigned verses for each day, with a question to start discussion; stories can be added for the children. The families are encouraged to spend up to five minutes each day reading the assigned passage and discussing the question, usually at meal time. This forces adults and children out of a passive learning role, so prevalent in churches today. It encourages family heads and potential teachers to apply God's Word first to their own family.

This family focus is a powerful tool for training and mobilizing new group leaders and elders/pastors. Many heads of families take turns teaching during Sunday worship, simply leading discussion on the same Bible passages they have been discussing with their families during the past week. We develop as leaders those men who shepherd their families and are active in evangelism of their friends. As people are added to the church, those who brought or initially befriended them are taught to take responsibility to ground them in the faith. We have developed materials to help young believers shepherd newer believers into the community. These who bring in new ones learn to shepherd; leadership develops naturally around these discipleship chains. Men shepherd their wife and other men; women shepherd women. Discipleship "chains" thus come into existence along relational lines.

These emerging leaders bring new believers through repentance, baptism, and preparation for "covenanting" (agreeing formally with the other members of the church to work and worship together with them in loving harmony and in obedience to Christ). Older leaders often phase out as these new ones phase in, take a coaching role only as they dedicate themselves to starting another church. Of course they can "do it better," but if they do, the newer ones will never learn. (The newer ones may surprise you too!)

27. **Implementation:** Mark items in Appendix E *Items to Review,* for further action (as a check list). Also file plans under the corresponding activities in your ARFs. Note here your general plans for discipling:

_____

_____

_____

_____

_____

Now you do what I say!
I fly over you
in this organization!

5. Obeying Jesus' Command to Love

<u>Recommended Bible Study, Luke 10:25-37.</u> Look for what God counts as real Christian love--born of faith and a proper relationship with him.

28. Enable potential leaders to develop their own ministries without fearing those who are over them.

Churches normally reproduce more readily in an atmosphere of freedom. Our Lord warned us against over-controlling (Matthew 20:25-28). If you are a leader, we encourage you to examine your leadership style. How great a need the church has for its leaders to humbly encourage the meaningful growth and ministry of every member of the body! Yes, immature members make many mistakes as we give them opportunities to grow in ministry. But remember the failures Jesus allowed his disciples to make, as well as the normal ups and downs of our own children as they develop. Failure and experimentation are a natural part of development. We urge you not to fear failure, either on your part or on the part of those you are training. We should rather be concerned that they learn from their failures and not ours.

Scoggins relates what he has learned about "leadership from within:"

We had to learn to make an important distinction: does a man (or woman) seek to serve because he is interested in self-promotion, or because he is discerning the call of the Holy Spirit on his life? Motives are central in Christian service (see 1 Cor. 3:10-15, 4:6). We found that leadership from within is a better model for leadership in the church. When the pastors/elders take a servant-leadership position within the flock--not over it--they get to know the people, as the shepherds of old did (as opposed to the ranchers in some of today's churches). They serve as examples of dying to self as they discern what is pleasing to the Lord, and are in a better position to discern the spirits of the people as they seek the Lord's will for themselves and for the church. Close relationships are necessary in order to help members see the hidden motives of their hearts and thus be protected from their own selfish motives in "spiritual service." Many a sincere saint has been destroyed by hidden, carnal motives in their service to the king.

We found that leadership from the top down tends to control and thus limit the avenues through which the Holy Spirit can speak and work. Leadership from within, in contrast, encourages individual initiative and thus broadens the avenues through which the Holy Spirit can speak and work in the church. Leadership that is close to the sheep is also better able to discern the dangers that come through carnal motives. Although it is seldom able to predict very far into the future the direction the Spirit is leading, leadership from within is much better able to discern the dangers as they creep up. Such leadership is essential for spontaneous reproduction of churches.

The New Testament emphasizes what we might call servant leadership. Jesus warned us against exercising authority for the purpose of control; human authority exercised "from the top down" violates the command of Jesus (Matt. 20:25-28). It inhibits church reproduction as quickly as anything. Such top-down control assumes that God will lead the church only through those presently in leadership. It leaves the so-called laity behind in passivity, since they must wait until the leader comes down from the mountain with a revelation from God as to what they should do, rather than taking responsibility before the Lord to seek to do their part. It kills individual initiative and limits the avenues through which the Holy Spirit can speak to the church.

Patterson also relates how he learned to build organization structure on loving relationships:

At first, in our work in Honduras, leaders felt they had authority simply because they were "above" others in the organization. When we began more biblical methods of discipling, we saw that the exercise of authority should come within the context of loving relationships. We kept the organizational structures for the sake of order but taught our people to place the authority of man-made organizations at a lower level than that of the authority of Christ's commands. We taught our people to let their authority grow out of loving relationships (note Jesus' comment in John 14:15, "If you love me, obey my commands"). I learned that if my disciples love me and know that I am helping them have a more effective ministry, they will do what I say, even though I have no organizational or political authority over them. We taught our people that for the sake of order their organizational authority might be defined by the constitutions of our churches and their regional associations, but it was not be based on them. The more traditional pastors kept rewriting their constitutions and bylaws to maintain positions of control. They complained that the regional church associations would undermine their power to exert discipline if we questioned their authority as national leaders. "Things will grow out of our control and we will have pure confusion," they insisted.

Our workers grew weary again of the criticisms, and we held another meeting. We prayerfully examined the Word to find God's basis for Christians and churches to relate to each other. We agreed to imitate the apostolic church in Jerusalem. It began at once to practice loving fellowship, evidenced in caring for one another in a material way (Acts 2:42-47). Our organization and fellowship, family ministries, and mercy ministries grow out of Jesus' command to love, rather than our man-made bylaws.

This did not bring confusion as the older pastors had prophesied but visibly strengthened the regional organization that was emerging among our new churches. We soon saw that our regional directors had far more influence and discipline by building their authority on loving relationships than did those who ruled with a doubled fist.

29. Start from the beginning to disciple a new believer with love and personal interest.

New believers feel that they are accepted by God only when we (the church) accept them in love. A newborn infant thrives on its mother's love but in later years is stunted in its social adjustment if its mother's love was lacking. Likewise, newborn Christians in the church are stunted spiritually, often permanently, if they are not lovingly discipled immediately after conversion. Scoggins relates:

If a church is going to grow and reproduce, it must find ways to integrate newcomers into the life and heart of the church. Our experience with some churches is that it often takes months, and sometimes even years, for newcomers to sense that they have become an insider in an established church. One way to avoid this is to teach our people to see each newcomer as a door to a new social circle that God might add to the church. The person who brings the newcomer should immediately begin to shepherd the person in the basics of the faith. If that person does not know how, we must show them. Newcomers are also trained to share their faith at once with their own social circle so that it is penetrated for the gospel. We have seen several cases where a whole network of friends and relatives is thus harvested for the kingdom. We have watched new churches be born because of such a harvest, and others where the entire social circle was added to an already existing church with dynamic results. We must avoid extracting a person from his or her social circle into the church before we try to penetrate that circle for the sake of the Kingdom.

Since some newcomers simply show up at the church, we should ask some members to be on the lookout for them and begin at once to befriend them and to shepherd them in the basics of the faith. Such a "Barnabas ministry" (Acts 9:26-28) is essential to the healthy growth and reproduction of the church.

30. Help new believers immediately to care for the needy.

The church in Jerusalem took care of its needy people from the start; in Acts 6 they named deacons to coordinate this work. From the very beginning we teach new believers to obey the greatest commandments (love God with all our heart and our neighbor as ourselves). We are to do good to all men, starting with the family of God (Gal. 6:10; 1 John 3:16-18). We help converts to begin at once to show their love for God and their neighbor in a practical way (Luke 10:25-37), teaching them that they have been saved to serve (Gal. 5:13). Each one has something to offer the believing community and his or her unsaved "neighbor."

We must avoid a self-centered approach to discipleship that gives new believers the idea that God's main interest is to save them from their sin and to meet their needs, so that they can be more prosperous and comfortable. Rather, we teach them that spiritual healing results in greater servanthood. Everyone who has the Holy Spirit has been given something to give others. We certainly do receive much when we become part of God's living community, but our motive is to give, not to get. Anything we receive should be seen not as what we deserve but rather as an undeserved gift of pure grace. Likewise, our responsibility is to give freely. Caring for the physical needs of others is the most basic way in which believers can show their true love for God (Luke 10:25-37).

We must provide new believers opportunities to practice simple acts of love and mercy before they are entrusted with the more influential ministries of teaching and leading. Much damage has been done in the church by those who have not been taught to love in a sacrificial way but who nevertheless rise to positions of teaching and leading without understanding the basics of love and compassion. Spiritual gifts that are helpful for cultivating practical love to heal broken relationships and physical sickness, deal with poverty, and cultivate edifying relationships between workers include compassion, giving, helps, service, and hospitality.

31. In poverty areas, combine church planting with community development.

Good development work done in Christian love normally requires persons with the following spiritual gifts:

Compassion. In poverty areas church planting is often combined with mercy ministries or small businesses. (Do not confuse mercy with mere pity that gives help in a way that creates dependency.)

Prophecy. Among people of limited education or radically different culture, this gift may call for using creative and artistic methods of communication of God's messages. (The biblical prophets, for example, often used the medium of poetry.)

Giving. Your team may need a businessman whose capital maintains a business that provides employment for the team.

Healing and casting out demons. Especially in pioneer fields where Satan has had complete control of the people's minds for centuries and they hold a world view incompatible with Christianity, God often brings about conversion through healings and signs, even among missionaries who are not from churches that normally deal with these gifts.

32. For continued, healthy church reproduction, let the Holy Spirit harmonize the use of different spiritual gifts in love.

To mobilize church members in ministry, we emphasize integration of ministries in the power of the Holy Spirit, not isolation of ministries as separate programs or departments. Scripture repeatedly emphasizes using the gifts in the body in loving harmony through the Holy Spirit.

Typically, Western churches compartmentalize their ministries, separating neatly between evangelism programs, Sunday schools, community work, worship, pastoral training, and so forth. This Western style of church organization tends to form areas of "turf." A church body is broken up into separate programs (with little cooperation between them) in which certain individuals gain influence and power. Often, simply maintaining their power within that program becomes the important thing. Attempts to remove the person or reduce the budget of the program develop into a cold war (and sometimes even into a hot split). Once such turf has been defined and begins to be protected, it becomes resistant to change, regardless of what the Holy Spirit might say. Such organization hinders the Spirit's work, since "God is opposed to the proud, but gives grace to the humble." Such organization fails to promote humility, forbearance, or cooperation on the part of every member of the body, which are needed for its edification by harmonizing, or balancing, its different gift-based ministries in love (Eph. 4:11-16).

In a missionary effort, the modern Western tradition of church organization may bring efficiency but not balance. For example, for church reproduction in poor, pioneer fields, the biblical style of organization is essential because effective church planting is normally united with poverty work and pastoral training. This interaction or networking between the gifts is necessary for the body to be healthy and balanced. Such networking cannot be contrived or controlled without doing violence to its ability to meet needs as they arise. Once again the advantages of leadership from within become apparent.

33. To discover and develop spiritual gifts most effectively (especially apostolic and pastoral gifts), *release potential leaders to work with new churches and small groups.*

<u>Recommended Bible Story:</u> Exodus 18:13-27. Look for why we establish elders over small groups and their leaders.

The apostles' two strongest passages on love (Rom. 12 and 1 Cor. 13) are both parts of exhortations to use different spiritual gifts in harmony. We can put most of a church's members to work if we help them discover their gifts in small group ministry where loving relationships are being formed.

We help members to detect and use their gifts in a small body in several ways. These include:

✔ *Join ministry or evangelistic groups in which they use their spiritual gifts to minister both to the unsaved community and to each other.* Converts are more easily discipled (followed through) if they are assimilated immediately, even before conversion into new small groups or churches.

✔ *Start or join new home groups or churches.*

✔ *Add ministries to existing Bible study groups,* to deal with felt needs and opportunities for witnessing or serving others. This is done in different ways. Some Bible study groups bring people together who have the same gift, for a specialized ministry, and invite people with a common need to their Bible study. Other shepherding groups minister to communities or families with different needs and bring together different gifts in the spirit of Romans 12:3-8, including that of teaching the Word. Some churches' Bible study groups all follow the same curriculum together. They study the same passages and follow the same guidelines for applying God's truths to their lives. This enables the coordinator of the groups to make sure that they maintain a satisfactory level of discipleship and balance in their application of the Word.

✔ *Add separate ministry groups that meet apart from the Bible study groups.*

✔ *Develop children's ministries and arrange for them to minister to their parents and each other.*

✔ *Name persons with a loving, helping disposition to disciple newer Christians on a personal or family basis.* This is normally done easier in the context of small groups, especially new small groups. Remember, the apostolic churches met in homes (see Acts 2:46; 5:42; 20:20; Rom. 16:3-5).

✔ *Seek to awaken and practice the most edifying gifts.* What is most edifying depends in part upon current needs and circumstances.

The gifts listed below generally assure that a group builds its organization on loving relationships and grows in knowledge of Christ, through conversions and in ministries:

Leadership. All ministry oriented groups need someone with the gift of leadership.

Evangelist. Most groups should do the work of an evangelist, and need at least one person with this gift to stimulate and furnish a model for the others.

Pastor/elder. Shepherding groups need at least one person who uses the pastoral gift. This gift is best used together with the pastor/elder gift, by the same person or by another who works closely with a pastoral type. If we use the gift of teaching by itself, we seldom shepherd the group in an edifying way. We also distinguish between the gift of teaching and the responsibility to teach. For instance, fathers are commanded to "bring up their children in the discipline and instruction of the Lord" (Eph. 6:4). They are required to teach their children in their home whether they are gifted as teachers or not.

As to teaching in the home, Scoggins reports:

Our experience is that as a head of a family carries out his God-given responsibility to teach, his giftedness will become apparent. Even if he is not gifted, he is still required to carry out his responsibility to teach his family, for which God will give him grace. Because of this, we train our members who are heads of families in the basics of teaching, at least for family devotions.

In addition to gifts of leadership, evangelist, pastor/elder, and teacher, special gifts are helpful for specialized ministries. Some groups specialize in marriage or family counseling. Others deal with drug or alcohol abuse recovery, overcoming grief, or other specific problems. Some deal with the needs of singles, elderly, or some other well-defined category of people. These groups need persons with the gifts of *exhortation, discernment, compassion,* or *helps.*

Many groups pray for the unsaved, the sick, and the hurting, for which the gifts of *faith, healing, casting out demons,* or other "sign gifts" are needed.

Groups doing community development need persons with the gifts of *discernment, giving,* or *compassion.*

Most ministry groups meet in homes, for which the gift of *hospitality* is needed.

When the elders or group leaders meet together, they often need to correct trends or errors, for which the gifts of *wisdom, prophecy, discernment,* and *leadership* are useful.

Groups ministering cross-culturally need the gift of *apostleship* (missionary).

On a pioneer mission field teams must train pastors and need at least one instructor with the gift of *teaching.*

> **Add plans in your ARFs to harmonize the gifts in love and in the power of the Holy Spirit, in a way that most members of your churches have an effective ministry. Helpful Bible passages are Romans 12, 1 Corinthians 12-14, and Ephesians 4.**

34. Detect and care for personal or family needs in small, loving groups.

Take advantage of the smallness of cell groups, house churches, and new congregations for dealing with personal and family needs (Ex. 18:24-26). Home groups enable elders to deal with personal needs, pray for each member, and help all to participate. They enable believers to have a ministry of caring. Mobilize as group leaders (elders) only loving persons who will take time to care--

Balanced Discipling
Triangle

usually men already very busy. Scoggins relates:

> In our experience with house churches men who will take time to care will come to the surface as they are given opportunity to do so. Some will come of their own volition, and many of these surprise us. But with proper discipleship and care, many who are at first reluctant to lead make radical changes in their lives in such a way as to become effective elders. Some require a challenge to consider if God has indeed called them to give their lives to the calling of a shepherd. This is done with great care and prayer, realizing that the call is from God, and the individual weighs the cost and the call before the Lord, to determine if he is able and willing to follow. This response often begins in the home; we have a great opportunity to detect potential leaders by seeing how men shepherd their families. A call to shepherd normally shows itself in one's own family.

35. For organization that reproduces, do *balanced discipling.*

Some teachers' academic orientation to ministry centers so much around the content of what they teach that they concentrate only on the meaning of the biblical doctrine as they teach, not on the task or the people. We help them to discipline themselves to integrate the Word, the work, and caring relationships in their teaching.

Think about how the Persons of the Trinity relate to each other. One does not exist, nor even work, without the involvement of the other. Similarly, the three primary dimensions of discipling must also be harmonized: loving **relationships** (growing out of our relationship with God the Father: "God *is* love") the **Word** (God the Son is the eternal, living Word, the very image of the Invisible God) and the **task** (God the Holy Spirit who empowers us for His work).

We might let the three sides of a triangle represent these three essential dimensions of balanced, reproductive discipling. Disciplers teach the Word with a task orientation (always equipping Christians for ministry), through loving relationships. The Holy Spirit uses both the Word and loving care to mobilize the hearers of the Word to become doers.

The *love* side refers to good relationships, including a loving relationship with God and with each other. It grows out of mature Christian character and the fruit of the Holy Spirit (Gal. 5:22-23). The base represents the *Word*, or what we teach. The final side signifies the *task*, or what God wants us to do.

Some seminaries emphasize the *Word* almost exclusively. They give little or no attention to a student's present pastoral work (the task), nor to developing loving relationships. Traditional professors seldom adapt teaching to students' fieldwork or take personal responsibility for their present ministry.

Some churches emphasize *loving relationships* almost exclusively. The congregation neglects the Word and the work, becoming ingrown and stagnant. Few obey Jesus' commands, other than loving one another.

Some mission agencies and church planting teams put almost exclusive emphasis on the *task*. Their workers burn out, neglect their families, and leave their coworkers feeling bruised.

Balanced discipling is normally reproductive, provided we integrate the three sides of the triangle. Do not simply *add* equal portions of all three aspects of discipling. Concentrate on how they produce one another. For example, teach in a way that mobilizes your disciples for the task, as you take loving, personal responsibility for the effective ministry of your disciple.

36. **Implementation:** Write below your general plans for your people to disciple others with genuine love, including when training leaders. Also, mark applicable items in Appendix E. As soon as possible, add all these plans to your *Activity Review Files*.

_____

_____

_____

_____

_____

_____

_____

_____

_____

_____

_____

_____

_____

_____

_____

6. Obeying Jesus' Command to Break Bread

<u>Recommended Bible Study, Matthew 26:26-28.</u>
Note Acts 2:42-46; the new converts in the first church in Jerusalem started immediately to break bread. Also see John 6; 1 Corinthians 10:1-4, 16-18; 11:18-34.

37. Glorify Jesus Christ by remembering Him with the ceremony He gave us to do so.

With regular, obedient celebration of the Lord's Supper, God develops a disciplined body in communion with Christ, one that is healthy and thus more ready to multiply. In pioneer fields where new workers so often lead new churches in homes, such a celebration of the Lord's Supper brings a seriousness and authenticity to the worship.

Scoggins recounts his discovery of the value of the Lord's Supper for new churches:

We found in Rhode Island that the celebration of the Lord's Table is very valuable for new churches. We encourage the churches to continue to strive to find new ways to make the celebration meaningful. Too often we fall into ruts, and the meaning of the celebration is lost. Often we celebrate it as part of an event of importance for the church community. One favorite event is when new members are being "covenanted" into the church. Another such event is when we send members off to start a new congregation. When two or more of our churches meet together is also a good time. We may celebrate it on a Sunday meeting or at a midweek meeting when we do not expect many unbelieving visitors.

We often have the Lord's Table around a fellowship meal. Sometimes we do it at the beginning of the meal, other times at the end. Still other times we have the bread at the beginning and the cup at the end, symbolizing our communion with the Lord throughout the meal.

The church may authorize any man who is a covenanted member to officiate the Lord's Table. Obvi-

Hey, them converts are too new to take Communion yet!

They'll think it's magic or something!

Quiet.

Their first concern is to obey Jesus.

We don't glorify Him when we neglect Communion.

ously, if the man has had no previous experience, the procedure will be reviewed with him by someone more experienced. We consciously avoid a single pattern, preferring a "menu" approach in which the person officiating the celebration can prayerfully consider different options to make the experience meaningful.

Patterson also recounts his struggle to enable new churches to benefit from the Lord's Supper:

At first, our new churches in Honduras seldom celebrated the Lord's Supper—only when a missionary or ordained pastor was present. But to receive God's fullest blessing they had to obey Jesus' command to break bread. As long as they neglected it, they could not take their worship as seriously as they should. So we adapted ordination requirements to the culture, authorizing elders in our pastoral training program to officiate the Lord's Supper, under the authority of experienced pastors.

The leaders of our national association rushed to our area for an emergency session. They voted not to recognize the lay pastor's licenses we gave to biblically qualified elders; these were no longer permitted to serve the Lord's Supper. One lay pastor stood to speak but tears filled his eyes; he took his lay pastor's license from his pocket, tore it up and threw the pieces on the floor, then walked out of the meeting without a word. He also walked out of the pastorate and out of his church, a crushed man.

I vowed it would never happen again. We met again with our workers and affirmed in prayer that we would obey Jesus above all else, even before the rules and majority vote of our national association of churches. Our churches began regularly obeying Jesus' command to "do this in remembrance of me." Some used a Baptistic, non-liturgical style; others a more formal, Lutheran style. All came to take it seriously. I rejoiced to see them discover profound worship in the mystery and the presence of Christ in the Eucharist.

38. Avoid excessive fear of allowing too much—or too little—of the *mystery* in Communion services.

By "mystery" we mean the invisible work of the Holy Spirit as he strengthens our unity with Christ and his body through partaking worthily of the consecrated bread and wine—that is, with a vital faith, having examined ourselves, as Paul commands, to confess our sins.

Some missionaries fear to let new churches break bread simply as the apostles did in Scripture and with the same respect for its mystery. This fear—whether we fear too much sacramental emphasis or too little—brings about human rules, limitations, and definitions that weaken the mystery. Where does this fear come from? Churches with theological roots in a more superstitious age tend to define the mystery of the Eucharist so speculatively or specifically that their pastor becomes a sort of magician. Their new churches, especially in pioneer fields, often neglect the Eucharist because they lack persons approved to officiate it. Churches with roots in a more rationalistic age tend to deny the supernatural work by the Holy Spirit in the Eucharist; their new churches neglect it because they find no real spiritual value in it.

Satan uses the fears arising from both extremes; church planters from both sides of the debate on sacrament versus symbol only are apt to say, "Our Lord says, 'This is my body,'" and "Yes, we must eat it in remembrance of him--but...." Then come exegetical acrobatics that force their fears on Scripture and their people. These fears are highly contagious. They keep both liturgical and non-liturgical leaders from simply trusting the Holy Spirit himself to illuminate the minds of their people as they examine with childlike, unprejudiced faith what God says in his Word about the Eucharist (such passages as John 6:26-69; 1 Cor. 10:2-4, 16-17; 11:23-34). Their churches are sometimes born already somewhat apostate, in that they are forced by human rules to disobey Jesus' command to break bread. They therefore miss its God-given blessing.

39. For communion that leaves us knowing we have really worshiped, even in a small house church, *invite the Holy Spirit to work powerfully* through this ceremony that Jesus instituted.

Sometimes we leaders must keep still and let the consecrated bread and wine speak for themselves through the power of the Holy Spirit and not turn the ceremony into another teaching time. If we seldom see tears of repentance and joy, we are not letting God make his own impact. Jesus ordained it for us to remember him and encounter his presence in a stirring, edifying way, enabling us with our physical senses to recall our sins and his blood sacrifice to forgive them. This communion lasts longer than the ceremony itself; throughout the week we remain in that conscious oneness with Christ and his body that the ritual so powerfully proclaims.

Patterson remembers his struggle to escape prejudices against "liturgy" that he took to Honduras:

I winced as a poorly educated village pastor served a rather large amount to drink for Communion, and without the usual warnings and explanations. "I'll have to straighten him out," I thought. Then I noticed the tears. Poor, illiterate campesinos lingered long over the cup, some with eyes closed in meditation. I had never seen such a united, contrite spirit around the Lord's Table! What had I missed? I did much praying as I looked again at what the apostles taught and practiced. Like most who prefer the word "ordinance" to "sacrament," I felt uneasy when anyone experienced anything mystical; I feared superstition distorting the ceremony instituted by Christ. But a suspicion kept creeping back--in this present rationalistic age, is not the greater danger to resist the supernatural aspect? I compared churches that enjoyed the mystery of the Eucharist with those that played it down. In Honduras, our churches were healthier when they celebrated it with its drama and mystery intact. And in America I recalled so many who left our churches that allowed no mystery in worship to seek it in more liturgical churches, or churches that allowed more feeling during times of praise, or even in false cults.

In non-liturgical churches I had heard--and given--

many warnings against sacramentalism in the Lord's Supper. But I reread the apostles' words in 1 Corinthians 10 and 11. Did he not warn rather against failing to recognize the mystery? Had I been overreacting against abuses in some liturgical churches? Was I basing my theology on negative experience rather than the Word of God? Was I keeping my disciples from "discerning the body" (1 Cor. 11:29-32)? I had been asking, "Discern which body?" The church as a body, or the bread as a symbol of Christ's physical body? But the mysterious unity of the two were precisely what the celebration affirmed. Paul wrote, "And is not the bread that we break a participation in the body of Christ? Because there is one loaf, we, who are many, are one body, for we all partake of the one loaf" (1 Cor. 10:16-17). I had pitied Christian married couples who failed to appreciate God's supernatural work in uniting them as one flesh and its mysterious connection with the union between Christ and his church (Eph. 5:25-32). Yet I had failed to see that Christ and his apostles taught the same type of mystery in our supernatural union in the body of Christ in the Eucharist!

I turned to my church history books and found no consolation; for virtually all churches, including those started by the apostles, until modern times, the Eucharist had been the core of their worship. Until quite modern times, no church, apart from short-lived, heretical splinter groups, whether Protestant, Catholic, or Orthodox, conceived of worship without the Lord's Supper as its climax. Long after the Protestant Reformation even non-liturgical churches kept the table for the Lord's Supper, or a kneeling rail to serve it, in the central position in the front of the sanctuary; the pulpit remained off to one side. In modern, Western, humanistic societies, churches began to give the central position to the pulpit instead of the altar, a custom which has now become the norm for most non-liturgical evangelical churches.

I also observed stronger discipline in churches that emphasized regular Communion. They corrected unruly members in humility and love, while other churches fell back into an Old Testament mentality of legalistic enforcement of rules or failed to discipline altogether except for gross sexual immorality.

After years of reflection I encouraged our churches to follow the apostles' model for the Lord's Supper as they found it in Scripture, avoiding human biases one way or the other. No church got carried away or lapsed into the superstition of transubstantiation, as some critics had predicted. It was a blessing, as though an ailing body found a vitamin it had been missing.

How often should a church celebrate Lord's Supper? Liturgical churches celebrate Holy Communion each week; this practice was mentioned, although not commanded, in Acts 20:7, and was typical of virtually all churches (Catholic, Orthodox and Evangelical) throughout history until several centuries after the Reformation. Even non-liturgical churches in pioneer fields, where they lack experienced preachers and worship leaders, may celebrate the Lord's Supper weekly for the first year or so, to assure that the people experience serious, edifying worship and encounter God at least once a week. Many--perhaps most--evangelical churches, in an effort to avoid Communion becoming mere mechanical ritual, celebrate it only once a month.

40. To bless God and receive his blessing, *practice all vital parts of worship.*

A new church in a pioneer field must set apart a definite, regular time for serious worship, even if it still has only a handful of members. Patterson discovered the importance of this:

When meeting in a home that lacked the worship atmosphere of a chapel, we needed to do something to convert the room into a temporary sanctuary. It helped to have a definite beginning and end to the worship; often we started with a call to worship during which we stood while someone invoked the Lord's presence and blessing. Sometimes we simply stood while the hostess brought the bread and wine of the Lord's Supper and placed them in the center of the room. On occasion the leader donned a simple vestment (usually a simple surplice--like a tie without a knot--laid over the shoulders) or used some other visible symbol. This helped particularly when we started worshiping with very few people. Sometimes we started in a home with only three or four converts long before the church started inviting the public. On occasion only I and the first convert were present when a church in embryo first met to celebrate the Lord's Supper.

During the main weekly worship celebration, do the following essentials for group worship.

Essentials for Group Worship

✔ **Pray**

✔ **Praise**

✔ **Teach** the Word of God

✔ **Confess** and **give assurance** of forgiveness

✔ **Celebrate Communion** (the Lord's Supper)

✔ **Give** (some churches simply provide an offering box, usually by the door)

✔ **Fellowship**

✔ (House churches especially) **A definite beginning and end to the worship time** (let the people know when the place ceases to be a living room in a private home and becomes a sacred sanctuary, and when it becomes a home again.)

These acts may be combined; for example, we might combine three of them by reading the *Word* to *praise* the Lord in *prayer*. Confession or assurance, as well as Bible teaching, might also be sung, chanted, prayed, read from Scripture, or acted out dramatically. Many liturgical churches follow a church calendar and forms that provide for a wholesome variety of combinations.

41. **Use the special spiritual gifts that God gives to certain people to help others praise him in a way that pleases him and blesses us.**

Wise pastors/elders seek those with the gifts of discernment of spirits, prophecy, faith, and exhortation. Tongues are also used in worship, especially during prayer time, by charismatic and Pentecostal churches; 1 Corinthians 14 requires that they be interpreted and spoken in order.

42. **For more effective worship and evangelism, deal conscientiously with *special seasons and holidays*.**

Many people more readily receive Christ or make serious commitments during special times such as Advent and Christmas, Lent and Easter. Other national holidays should also be celebrated by adapting them to Christian worship. Keep an eye on the church year with its seasons, as well as on national holidays, for special emphases in worship.

Evangelicals in the West often neglect the seasonal celebrations of our faith. Roman Catholicism and Eastern Orthodoxy have many celebrations and feasts. Both the Old and New Testaments affirm seasonal celebrations. Some Protestants overreact against pagan influences in Catholicism by emptying their Christian faith of nearly all seasonal celebration. Some churches consider it spiritual to avoid happy celebrations. They retain only a gray, overcast faith where expressions of joy and deep feeling are suspect. Most young people are repulsed by such an unnatural asceticism, and perhaps our Lord is too. He certainly took the Jewish festivals seriously and was accused of being a winebibber (NIV: "drunkard") and partying with sinners and their crowd. Mature faith certainly has its reverent and austere aspects, but there is joy and celebration as well, on earth as in heaven. Scoggins remarks:

We try to mark special occasions with feasts. These include when a new church begins and when a new member is covenanted in (he or she is the guest of honor, of course). Weddings, and reminders of key dates in the life of the churches can also be the basis for feasting and celebration.

43. **Implementation:** Mark items that you want to apply to your work in *Appendix E*. Note below general plans for Communion:

_____

_____

_____

_____

_____

_____

_____

_____

_____

_____

_____

_____

7. Obeying Jesus' Command to Pray

Prayer has great psychological benefits.

But to get things done, we need big dollars.

Get thee behind me!

SAINT JAMES CHURCH

<u>**Recommended Bible Stories, Genesis 18:16-33; Matthew 26:36-46.**</u> Look for guidelines for intercession and submission to God.

Scoggins relates how he learned spiritual warfare as churches began to multiply:

Our experience has been that prayer partnerships that last from several months to years are valuable in pulling down Satan's strongholds. Second Corinthians 10:4 talks about the weapons of our warfare being divinely powerful for the pulling down of strongholds. Certainly these include the strongholds in people's lives that cripple them from fulfilling God's plan to love one another. The newest believer needs to be trained in the use of the powerful weapon of intercessory prayer. The older believers need to have the weapon continually honed for battle through use on behalf of others. Prayers of intercession, praise, repentance, healing, and petition need to permeate our churches, both in public worship and in the quietness of two or three gathered together.

I remember how, in the early days of my walk with God, I met weekly for prayer with two other men. We would meet on a particular evening of the week, usually after the church prayer meeting. It was not uncommon for us to go long after midnight. The other two were further along than I, and I learned much about prayer from them. Often we would confess our struggles and our sins to one another, then have lengthy sessions of prayer. When we began new ministries, they would be bathed in much prayer. We covenanted to pray for each other every day of the week. We met together this way for over two years. It was probably the most significant thing that brought me out of my hermit's shell. I learned how to pray for others as well as be vulnerable in having people pray for me.

### 44.	Pray constantly for God's enablement to keep reproducing as a church.

The new converts in the church in Jerusalem began at once to pray fervently (Acts 2:42). Jesus commands his disciples to pray (John 16:24). An essential pastoral ministry that stems from Jesus' command to pray is to develop regular prayer by the church as a body and daily prayer by its members, individually and with their families. Church planting teams, especially in areas where Satan has held total control over the people's minds for centuries, need someone with the gift of faith. That person will encourage the rest to pray. The gifts of healing, miracles, and exorcism also depend on prayer.

Patterson also explains the place of prayer in their early Honduran ministry:

As is common for new missionaries, I wanted the church growth and multiplication to be considered a result of my ministry. God wanted it to be considered a result of his work. So he let me fail. And fail. I wanted control and recognition. God gave me failures. I finally prayed--and meant it--"Lord, I'm tired of failing. I don't care any more about my own ministry. Just let me help my disciples to have a good ministry." God answered that prayer. When my pastoral students saw that I was no longer using them to build my own empire but was trying to help them have an effective ministry, they began following my teaching conscientiously. I discovered a power and influence that I had lacked before--but only when I did not seek it.

Problems still came. I recalled with bittersweet relief that Paul associated the pains of starting new churches with those of childbirth. Many times I prayed for God's help to relinquish control and to escape from the worries involved. I had to keep giving the new churches back to God. I was a slow learner when it came to seeing how church growth and reproduction came not from our strategies for reproduction, our discipling, our teaching, or other efforts of ours. God waited for us to ask him for it! Paul planted, Apollos watered, but God gave the growth. He does not bless methods, only loving obedience undergirded with prayer.

45. Help your disciples to grow spiritually by developing their daily personal and family devotional life.

We are to pray without ceasing and to teach our people to do the same (1 Thess. 5:17). Every new believer should see family devotions modeled. We may need to name someone in each house church or small group to mobilize disciplers who show new believers and families how to have personal or family devotions.

46. Pray continually for the salvation of the lost and for a vision of normal church reproduction.

Together with your coworkers and team members, pray and plan for your church to use its own God-given potential to reproduce. For reasons that he alone knows, the all-powerful God limits what he does on earth to our faith and our requests. If we want sinners to be converted, we ask him to transform them. If we want our churches to multiply, we ask him for the miracle.

Jesus illustrated this potential for spontaneous growth and reproduction in his parables of the sower, the mysterious spontaneous growth, and the mustard seed (Mark 4). To disciple a large population or people group ("nation" in the biblical sense), we sow and cultivate the gospel so that churches, like plants, reproduce spontaneously in daughter and granddaughter churches.

cannot make it grow; we can only cultivate it, water it, and protect it so that it reaches its God-given potential. Calculate what would happen if we let a single grain of rice fall in "good soil" and reach its miraculous potential (as Christ said, up to a hundredfold) and then did the same with each of these new grains. In just a few years we could feed the entire human race with the grain reproduced from it. This is the way Jesus said his church would grow and reproduce. We cannot make the church grow. We sow, water, and cultivate it in faith; God gives the growth (1 Cor. 3:6). Every time we eat or even look at the grass and trees, we are enjoying the fruit of God's miraculous reproductive power. All creation keeps reminding us several times a day: "This is how God works!"

Like all other living things God has created, an obedient church has within itself its own seed to reproduce normally after its own kind, just like grain. Rice reproduces rice; cows reproduce cows; churches--Christ's living body on earth--reproduce churches. By faith the pastor, church planter, or evangelist taps a church's God-given power to reproduce in daughter and granddaughter churches.

Help your people to rely on this God-given power to reproduce. The first grain comes from a "mother church" as it sends its people to witness or reproduce daughter churches. We believe just as Abraham did (he is our model for saving faith) in the miraculous reproduction of God's people, that his descendants would be as numerous as the stars (Gen. 15:6; Gal. 3:6).

47. *Plan prayerfully* for continued growth and reproduction.

By faith we plan together to let the churches and groups multiply. A pastor who disciples newer pastors within his church taps God's power to reproduce churches by releasing his disciples to start and pastor new churches. In a pioneer field the first tiny congregation will grow and reproduce if the new disciple is taught loving, prayerful, faithful obedience. Plan for it! Pray for it! Work toward it!

Scoggins reports how he had to deal with new leaders as the churches started multiplying:

Often at this early stage of planning a pastor or church planter has to deal with his "flesh." Western culture worships success and efficiency. We fear failure and try to avoid it at all costs. As a result, new leaders tend to overcontrol, inhibiting the spontaneous leading of the Spirit through the flock.

God, in his wisdom, allowed me to be trained as a research scientist. Every researcher knows that for every successful experiment there are ninety-nine failures. Each failure is crucial because, when analyzed, it moves us further toward the successful one. When the success occurs, it is almost anticlimactic, since the failures have been pointing to it, defining it, like a loop being drawn tighter and tighter around what we are seeking to grasp. In other words, we learn more from our failures than our successes. This is true of both us and our disciples. We need to give them plenty of room in which to fail and need to show them how to evaluate their failures in light of God's sovereignty, helping them to see that every failure opens an opportunity for growth.

Another thing I learned from research is that, although a scientist starts with a hypothetical solution to a problem and progresses toward it, the real strides forward in science occur when supposedly forward progress is blocked and we try completely new ideas. This is frustrating, since it is unanticipated, and may take weeks, months, or years to discern the new directions to go. How many churches simply keep walking a treadmill to nowhere because they fear to try new directions? Instead of making radical changes, they somehow justify making the vital, reproducing Christian life into a routine of maintaining programs. And often even pastors back this mundane routine, praising the rut the church is running in, fearful of giving the congregation the flexibility to try new things (of which ninety-nine will fail) in order to restore the walk of faith. Where leaders desire to control the direction of the church, one can often predict where the church will be years from now simply by looking at where it is not going now. How sad that some churches allow the Holy Spirit, the supreme agent of change on the earth today, less flexibility than a scientist is allowed in a laboratory!

Certain forces beyond our control limit a church's potential for growth and reproduction. Work around these forces. Avoid fighting against them. For example, if it costs too much to rent or build for congregation, don't let this stifle your growth. Simply keep multiplying tiny new house churches. Other factors affecting growth include the people's responsiveness, population trends, an obsession for obtaining wealth, violent persecution by authori-

ties, poor mission management that restricts a missionaries' work, or difficulty in traveling from one community to another.

Church planters sometimes excuse a poor response by saying that the people are hard (poor soil), when in reality they simply need to multiply the kind of nuclei around which the growth can take place. Remember, "good soil" for starting a new church in a pioneer field is lots of bad people (Rom. 5.20: "Where sin abounds, grace does much more abound").

For too long some evangelical ministries have been competing against one another. Evangelists, church planting teams, pastors/elders, and pastoral trainers must cooperate much more closely, in the spirit of Ephesians 4:11-16, to help the church of Jesus Christ expand through reproducing churches. Also, many old and new churches need to shed their fears of one another in order to multiply their ministry. What can you do to harmonize your gifts with those of other ministries and churches? How will you convince your church(es) that they can tap God's power to grow and reproduce spontaneously? How will they begin to use their own inner, God-given power instead of relying on outside human resources, technology, or money? How will you get your people to pray for the miraculous power of God to reproduce? (Please record your plans in your ARFs.)

Does this mobilization to multiply seem like an impossible leap for you? Then help your people to pray that God will allow nothing to impede the free reproduction of new churches or small groups. We pray with our people for the Lord of the harvest to send laborers.

48. In keeping with the vision for ongoing growth and multiplication, *continually reproduce new leaders.*

Multiplying churches is almost synonymous with multiplying leaders. Churches normally grow and reproduce most rapidly by training leaders rapidly on the job. New churches often grow out of small evangelistic groups or home Bible studies with an evangelistic thrust, provided their leaders also receive pastoral training at the time the small group becomes a new church. As a church multiplies leaders to teach these evangelistic studies and to shepherd the sheep that come to Christ through them, it increases its ability to grow and reproduce.

If you are a leader in an inner-city church with a building available, you may simply reproduce evangelistic Bible study groups (sometimes called "discovery groups" or "fellowships") rather than separate daughter churches--provided you are working within your own ethnic group, economic level, and subculture. If you are in a multi-ethnic area, remember that God commands his church also to do cross-cultural evangelism (we are to witness for Jesus also in "Samaria"--Acts 1:8). If you plant a church in another ethnic group, be strongly cautioned to plant a separate church, with its own controlling elders. If you attempt to absorb them into your congregation, conflict will arise from cultural differences--always. If they are assimilated into your church's culture, your ability to evangelize that people group thoroughly is canceled (because your evangelism cancels their culture when successful--a self-defeating policy if we want a church to grow and reproduce in that culture). We must not extract people from their culture into ours but let them set up a congregation that will be able to penetrate their culture thoroughly.

The need to keep training new leaders in an apprenticeship discipling relationship with more experienced leaders becomes obvious when you seriously tap God's power to reproduce. As you organize your leadership training, do not forget that the church grows not only by addition (adding converts to an existing body) but also by reproduction (multiplying the small bodies to which converts are more easily added). Also remember that converts are far more likely to follow through if assimilated at once into a new group or church with other new Christians with whom they can identify.

Certain spiritual gifts are especially helpful for enabling churches to multiply through God's power; likewise, a church planting team needs persons who have these gifts:

Faith;

Evangelist--in the sense of Philip the evangelist, who presented Christ to people on a personal level;

Apostle--church planter, the "sent one," or apostle in the sense that Barnabas was an apostle who equipped new leaders in other cultures (Acts 14:3, 13-14);

Pastor/teacher (elder, shepherd)--to equip the saints for ministry.

49. **Implementation:** Mark applicable numbered items in *Appendix E*, for later review. Note your general plans now, to add to your ARFs later under activities on prayer and enabling a mother church to use God's power to multiply daughter churches. State below what you will do to tap God's power to grow and reproduce:

_____

_____

_____

_____

_____

_____

_____

_____

_____

_____

_____

_____

_____

_____

_____

_____

_____

8. Obeying Jesus' Command to Give

Recommended Bible Study, 1 Corinthians 9; 2 Corinthians 8 and 9. Look for principles of giving.

The first converts in Jerusalem started giving generously from the very beginning, as Jesus commanded (Acts 2:45). This giving no doubt did not just happen; like modern believers, they had to receive specific instruction. The apostles must have taught them to give, at once. The pastoral ministry of developing Christian stewardship grows out of Jesus' command to his disciples to give generously (Luke 6:38).

Scoggins explains how he had to present Christian stewardship in the new churches (which have been giving generously):

We are constantly challenging new believers who have worshiped at the alter of materialism to repent and consider that God may have a lower view of money than they do. We have seen several men change their highest priority from making money to making disciples. The result is usually a drop in their standard of living (and their giving to the church). We had to point out to them some basic principles; Galatians 5:13, for example, defines the Spirit-filled walk as an enslavement to one another motivated by love. New believers need to be taught that they have been saved to serve and that the norm is for them to look for ways to give rather than receive (2 Cor. 9:7). Indeed, the norm in the early church was to give what one had (Acts 2:42-47; 4:32-37).

Let those with lots of money pay God to work !

Jesus didn't say that about the poor widow.

Giving can be of time, effort, and money. For us in the West we tend to define giving only in terms of money, but we need to realize that to extend God's kingdom this may be the least important thing we give. Certainly Ephesians 4:11-16 emphasizes the giving of self (see 2 Cor. 8:5).

We also point out that the Lord himself dealt severely with those who gave for selfish motives (Acts 5:1-11). If giving wrongly was dealt with so severely, how much more will the Lord judge those who infiltrate the church with selfish motives, looking to receive rather than give? Church discipline is necessary in such cases, in order to protect the spirit of generosity (2 Thess. 3:6-15). This is another reason why it is important to define clearly who are the members of the church and what is expected of them (one purpose of covenanting when one joins the church).

50. To help converts escape the misery of severe poverty, teach them *sacrificial, voluntary stewardship* from the beginning.

Patterson recalls his struggle with stewardship among the very poor:

Like most missionaries, I started out being too generous with our American dollars. In time, even though the amounts were small, it caused much sadness and resentment within the ranks of our closest workers. Although we did not pay the pastors, we subsidized our extension teachers and other projects with funds from America. One of our most faithful workers became quite demanding of this help, not for himself, but for urgent needs of the very poor people in the villages where he was training pastors by extension. His demands were becoming forceful, and we felt that his influence was weakening our churches' sense of Christian stewardship. Being poor did not excuse them from obeying God's command to give. In fact, we saw over the years that those who gave sacrificially in love, in spite of their painful poverty, escaped from it. But those who gave little because of their poverty remained in it.

The showdown came when the worker demanded money for one of the pastors so that he could help with the extension teaching. I refused. He became furious, pointed his finger in my face, and shouted, "If those new churches fall, it will be your fault! I know you can get the money from the churches in the States. It will be your fault before God!"

I had to do something before his attitude spread to other workers. With great effort I replied, "If the churches' life depends on American money and not the Holy Spirit, then let them fall. And the sooner the better! If our work is built on American dollars, then we are deceiving ourselves."

It became evident, even in the most painfully poor areas, that those who gave sacrificially in their extreme poverty were able after a few years to get shoes for their children and educate them and to live healthily (although not in luxury, which God did not promise). But others who did not give to God's work because of their poverty, were--with no exceptions--left in their poverty. We came to see very plainly that even the poorest of churches, if they give sacrificially or tithe, soon meet their basic financial needs and their members escape from their painful poverty. We had to help these churches develop a realistic budget and emphasize that the treasurer could pay out *only* what was authorized in the budget. It was now obvious: we rob the poor of a blessing if we do not encourage them to give what they can. If they lack money, they can give products of the field or other things.

51. To avoid dependency or resentment, *fund church planting in poverty areas with extreme care.*

Probably nothing stifles the reproduction of churches in another culture more than outside funding. It carries a subtle form of control; a person who receives it feels morally obligated to do what the outsiders say, since they control the flow of the funds. We must warn of the danger of paying pastors with outside funds. Paying a pastor with inside funds can also stifle church multiplication if he is not a good steward. Paid pastors, more often than bi-vocational pastors or elders, discourage starting new churches nearby, even in affluent societies. Patterson recalls, "A Honduran pastor once warned me about helping *too much* with building programs or workers' expenses, 'A demon rides in on every dollar that comes from the United States.'"

Subsidizing new churches in any way from the outside, in any culture, can stifle giving by the local people. If the pastors are poor, they will soon want more. Satan whispers to them, "Why plant more churches? You do not receive enough help now as it is." Church multiplication is frequently paralyzed in the poorer countries where Americans and Europeans have been most generous. Both "tentmaker" and "full-time" paid Christian workers have the blessing of Scripture (Acts 18:1-5).

For church reproduction among very poor people, use non-funded, low budget or no budget programs--nothing beyond what local participants can provide. Let pastors start out being bi-vocational. Let new, poor churches have several unpaid elders (copastors) who share the pastoral responsibilities. Avoid institutional programs for churches and pastoral training. Steer clear of budget-oriented planning, high administration costs, dependency on buildings, paying for work rather than by calling on volunteers, professionalism, and building power through organizational politics.

Scoggins, who advises church planting teams in a poor North African field, reports:

The poverty in most third world fields presents a sharp, often painful, tension for Western missionaries. They usually have far more money than the local believers, even those that are well off by their standards. If they begin sharing their substance with the church, where will it end? The church becomes dependent on the missionary money. It inevitably attracts "rice Christians," who come not to give but to receive, thus undermining the cross-bearing discipleship mentality of the church.

We have found a similar problem in the United States. Since we start house churches with unsaved people (starting with two or three families), it usually takes some time for the wallets to get sanctified. If the church planters give to the church at that time, it gets a false sense of the financial resources available to it, and the church becomes dependent on outsiders. We encourage the missionary always to take a long-range view of what is best for the church.

My experience with missionaries working in third world situations is that they often experience guilt over having so much in comparison with their brothers in Christ. Certainly some may be moved by the Spirit to identify more closely with their target group by forsaking a higher standard of We have found it better with house churches not to support the elders financially. We encourage the support, however, of itinerant personnel who have a ministry with a network of house churches.

This is a faith work that requires faith on the part of the worker and does not strap any one church.

53. **Implementation:** Mark items by their number in *Appendix E* that you plan to deal with later. Also, please note your general plans below, for the churches to practice Christian stewardship and support their own workers:

_____

_____

_____

_____

_____

_____

_____

_____

_____

_____

_____

_____

_____

_____

_____

_____

_____

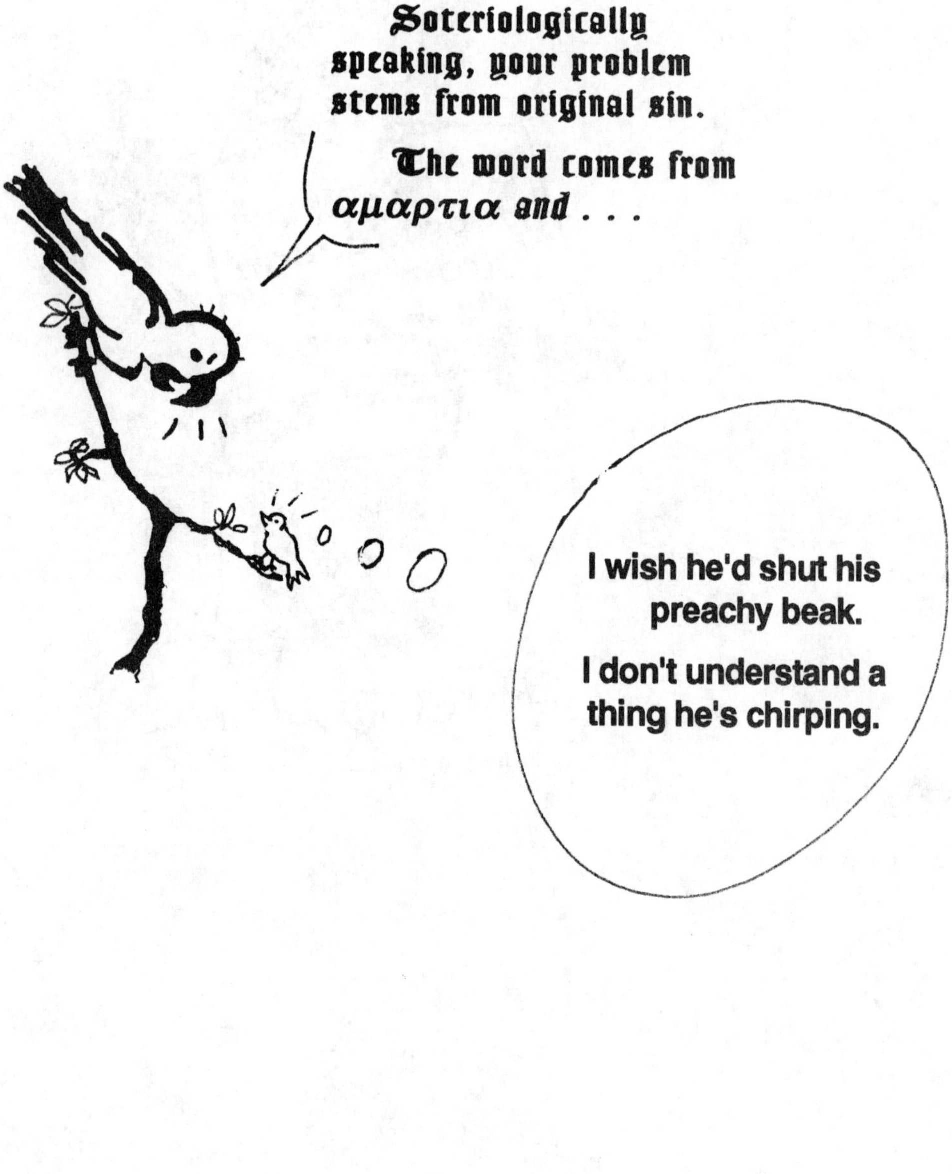
Soteriologically speaking, your problem stems from original sin.
The word comes from αμαρτια and . . .
I wish he'd shut his preachy beak.
I don't understand a thing he's chirping.

9. The Viewpoint of the Pre-Christian

Church reproduction principles are applied repeatedly in this guide to different ministries. Please look over all the ministries, but give close attention to the ones that apply to you or your coworkers. We begin in this chapter by considering church reproduction from the viewpoint of the pre-Christian.

<u>Recommended Bible Study: John 4</u>. Look for the type of person that is most likely to respond to the gospel (see also Luke 10:3-7).

Don't listen to those voices that say that church reproduction concerns only specialists in church planting! It's for all Christian workers. Let us look at it first from the viewpoint of the person who has the most to gain--or lose--from it: the *pre-Christian*.

From the outset, a movement for Christ among an unreached people needs evangelism that is culturally relevant. A good missionary is sensitive to anything that needlessly offends the people, in the way we worship or witness. Patterson recalls:

We found it hard to get Honduran men, especially heads of households, to attend church, let alone receive Christ. These macho peasants simply were not interested. They would observe the worship through a window, see a lot of women and children, shrug their shoulders, and walk away. How could we get these men--mature heads of families--excited about the gospel? How could we get them to talk about it to each other and their families? We had another meeting to discuss it. The Hondurans themselves furnished the answers.

We did several things, most of which brought renewed criticism from the old guard. We asked women not to take highly visible positions of leadership. We circulated doctrinal studies in the form of comic books. (This step brought the most complaints.) We switched to a more readable, modern version of the Bible. Perhaps most important was that we aimed at the homes, beginning our witnessing through the head of the household, as Peter did with Cornelius, and Paul with the Philippian jailer (Acts 10 and 16). Even before the men knew Christ, we asked them to repeat the Bible stories we told them, to their families and friends. (If we told the stories in their peasant style, they did not hesitate to repeat them.) Soon our churches had more men than women--something new for Honduras.

54. Prayerfully plan for a movement *of the people* for Christ.

A movement in which churches reproduce spontaneously grows out of a popular, grass-roots interest in the gospel of Jesus Christ. Wise church planters give attention to creative, often artistic, methods of awakening interest among pre-Christians. By "popular" we do not necessarily mean that people like it. But they are talking about it, often arguing about it. The people themselves, entire families, are concerned about the good news of salvation in Jesus Christ. They may reject it, but they are nevertheless concerned. The gospel becomes confidential news and travels along the same lines as gossip, between family and friends.

55. Do *incarnational* evangelism.

To multiply the nuclei (cores of groups) around which continued growth by multiplication takes place, *do not extract persons from their circle of family and friends to evangelize them on your turf* (that is, in your house or where you are in control). Jesus emptied himself of his divine glory and power to become a man and draw near to "publicans and sinners," eating and drinking with them. So we, too, evangelize on their turf, making ourselves vulnerable by witnessing where they are in control: for example, under the roof of an unconverted head of a household.

Church planters aiming at reproduction will do what they need to, to acquire this essential skill of incarnational evangelism. It is fundamental and universally applicable and should be mastered before trying the traditional Western or institutional approaches to evangelism. The incarnation of Jesus is our best example for identifying with those we are discipling for Christ. Remember, we also draw near to publicans and sinners and eat and drink with them as he did when he emptied himself of his divine glory and took on human flesh.

We imitate Jesus in this when we step outside of our church buildings and mission bases to work with the people (rather than putting on ever-bigger programs on our own turf to attract the people to us). We work within their existing family, culture, and social structures, rather than bringing them into our own organization in order to find Christ. We normally do this best by spending time with them in their homes, giving them a model for evangelizing that they can imitate immediately and pass on to their own people. Patterson recounts:

We found, when we penetrated a town for the first time with the gospel, that it was not always wisest to rent a room and invite the people to a place that we controlled, where we felt secure but they didn't. On Christmas Eve, for example, instead of inviting them to a celebration where we were staying, it was better to visit them in their homes. We made ourselves vulnerable, taking some cookies perhaps, or some other small token of friendship, to their house, rather than expecting them to respond to the invitation of an ''outsider'' to a religious meeting where their own friends and family would not be present and they might feel uncomfortable.

I finally saw what the missiologists meant when they talked about focusing on a particular people group and subculture. We were getting far better results when we kept new converts in a loving relationship with their unsaved, pagan friends, when we took Christ to them (instead of them coming to us) and started a new group or church within their own social circle. We no longer jerked each new convert out of his circle and transplanted him into a church made up of the church planting team members, or of others perceived as outsiders by the convert. We helped them to tell Bible stories about salvation and to witness to their own unsaved family members and friends about what Jesus had done for them.

Scoggins adds:

In Rhode Island we have found that men tend to warm up to a vision. There seems to be a pioneer spirit in men that needs to be stretched. From the outset of evangelism, we try to explain the vision God has for his Kingdom, its expansion, and their place in it. We find that men tend to be strongly drawn to such ''Kingdom'' evangelism. Perhaps this is the response Jesus points to in Matthew 11:12: ''From the days of John the Baptist until now, the kingdom of heaven suffers violence, and violent men take it by force.''

An example from physics has helped me explain this. Moving objects generate friction, which tends to slow down the object. It seems that there is a similar tendency in institutions that human beings develop. Certainly in the church there is a tendency toward maintenance activities as opposed to growth activities, which bring constant change. But Christ has given the church its marching orders: Advance! The Kingdom of heaven is at hand! From evangelism onward, we must present this God-centered call to those who would be his people if a vital reproducing Christianity is to be sustained.

56. Develop a doctrinal foundation for witnessing so that converts are converted to Jesus Christ and not just to the church.

<u>Recommended Bible Story: Genesis 6-9</u>. See also 1 Peter 3:12-22, Exodus 11-15, and 1 Kings 18.

In **chapters 6-9 of Genesis**, emphasize God's holiness as seen in the flood. The ark is a picture of Jesus' salvation (by faith we enter into the risen Christ the same way that Noah's family and the animals entered into the ark in order to be saved from God's punishment). We allow the Holy Spirit to use the Word of God to convince people of the danger of their sin before God, and the power of Jesus' death and resurrection to save them.

In **1 Kings 18**, emphasize the unity of the one true God, his wrath against idolaters, and what kind of modern idolatry corresponds to that of the prophets of Baal of that time.

In **Exodus 11-15**, emphasize God's desire to separate

his own people from Egypt and the godless world around them; recount his great power demonstrated in the miraculous crossing of the Red Sea.

If people believe in Jesus the same way Buddhists or Muslims believe in their faith--for cultural reasons only--they lack the Spirit of God. The best evangelists (i.e., the ones most often used by the Holy Spirit to bring about conversion) are normally the new believers. We show them how to explain to their family and friends that Jesus, God's Son, died and rose again to save us. They do not need to understand, at this time, details about how Jesus' death and resurrection save them and their friends; they need to believe it. And, for maximum assurance, they need to know that they have been born into a new, loving community. Having been forgiven, they enter into a whole new Kingdom. "For you once were not a people, but now you are the people [ethne] of God." As citizens of this Kingdom, we have responsibilities to its other citizens. We proclaim this relational aspect of salvation as an essential part of evangelism. The message of salvation incudes the purpose God has for us in salvation, namely strengthening and extending his Kingdom.

We witness with power when the Holy Spirit uses our words to convict people of their danger. The infinitely holy God cannot look upon sin. This appreciation of his absolute holiness starts with the fear of God. He is so good, and we so evil by comparison, that he must punish our sins (we do not teach holiness as simply another item in a list of God's attributes). Normally, pre-Christians see this point if we relate Old Testament stories in which God punished human sin.

57 Practice *reproductive witnessing* so that converts hear the gospel in a way that they can pass on immediately to others.

The easiest way to get converts to relate the gospel to their families and friends is to tell them easy-to-repeat stories. These would include the historical accounts of the gospel; for example:

In Matthew 27, relate *Jesus' death*;

In John 20-21, *Jesus' resurrection appearances.*

Other stories which help new Christians are:

Jesus' baptism (Matt. 3)

Jesus' temptation (Matt. 4)

Jesus' parables (Matt. 13; 25; Luke 10; 15; etc.)

Jesus' miracles (Mark chapters 1-10; John chapters 2; 6; 9; 11; etc.)

The items which follow contain keys to evangelize in a way that God normally uses in movements of church reproduction.

58. Communicate first the *essentials* of the gospel.

These are the *sacrificial death* of the Son of God, his *life-giving resurrection, forgiveness* of sins, and *eternal life for believers.*

59. *Pray regularly and fervently* for those we witness to.

60. Befriend and win the confidence of respected *heads of households*.

61. Help heads of households to evangelize their *families and friends*.

Encourage them to take responsibility for reaching their own extended social circle, to continue drawing near in love and faith, as Jesus did, to the lost, as that circle widens.

Scoggins explains:

One way we found to "infect" an entire family is to provide the head of the family with weekly reading schedules to read to the family. These schedules are quite simple; for each day a section of Scripture is indicated, along with a question for discussion. We usually print a four-weeks' schedule on a half-sheet of paper (two weeks on each side) so that if fits easily in the Bible. We encourage the man to read this during a meal time, before the plates are removed. He simply opens his Bible to the Scripture portion indicated and reads it. He then asks the question printed or another suitable discussion question that may come to him. A discussion can follow. He then closes in prayer. The whole thing takes only three to five minutes, but several healthy principles are being reinforced: the husband is taking the spiritual lead in the home; he is evangelizing the wife and children; he is learning how to bring up his children in the discipline and instruction of the Lord; he is learning the skill of teaching and shepherding in a family environment, which enables the church leaders to discern how he might minister in meetings of the larger church body.

62. In a new community share the gospel first with a *person of peace* (Luke 10:6).

This is a person whom God has already prepared, someone already respected in the community. God channels his good news through this contact (as Cornelius in Acts 10, Lydia and the jailer in Acts 16). Help such persons of peace to pass the gospel on immediately (even before they are saved) to their own family and friends. Do not separate converts from their friends or relatives (except in the case of drug addicts or alcoholics, from fellow addicts). We do not alienate them from their unbelieving friends in order to identify with a church made up of outsiders on our team.

63. Form a *new church or group* inside this circle of friends and relatives.

Keep the number of outsiders, including team members, to a minority at meetings during the birth phase of the new church. Scoggins explains:

If the husband is able to talk openly with his wife and children, we encourage him to begin a weekly Bible study at his house, where the reading schedule can be used and they can discuss God's Word at greater length. If he has friends or relatives who might come, we encourage him to include them in this "gathering meeting." It may help for the missionary or a member of the church planting team to attend also, but often it is better not to. Let the man do as much as he is able. Older believers should not be encouraged to come to these first "gathering meetings" unless they are bringing unbelieving friends or relatives. Once two or three have come to Christ, the group can be encouraged to start meeting as a community on Sundays. These "community meetings" will be where the life of the body is practiced, centered around the Lord's Supper; later other activities are added as needed.

64. Where meeting in large groups is illegal, *form several tiny groups* that can more easily avoid detection by authorities.

Two or three persons, to begin with, can meet for worship and Communion (Matt. 18:20; Acts 2:46-47).

65. Give ample *time* for the Holy Spirit to convince a family.

Present the gospel in a meaningful way several times before "shaking the dust off your feet." Most converts need to be hear about Jesus from five to seven times, often weeks apart, before the Holy Spirit enables them to receive him in their hearts. Scoggins explains:

In the case of Muslims, it is not unusual for conversion to take years. This requires perseverance as well as persistence. One prays for wisdom, as to how to continue to pursue a contact who is open. We usually avoid shaking the dust off our feet until the seeker shows evidence of rejecting the message. As long as progress is evident, we persevere. Even if there is rejection, we explain the way back by means of repentance. We encourage those engaged in this evangelism to pray to discern the spirit of the person we continue witnessing to, and to realize that we as Christians are the sweet odor of life to those who are saved, but the stench of death to the lost.

66. Help the head of a family to *affirm verbally the essential gospel truths* during each presentation of the gospel.

These are: the value of Christ's death, for himself and his family (forgiveness), and the value of Christ's resurrection, for himself and his family (new, pure, eternal life). When they believe, baptize the entire family. Scoggins affirms the results they find when they evangelize through the head of the household: "A husband normally precedes his wife and children in salvation and baptism; in this case he might be authorized by the elders to baptize his own family."

67. Do not push people into making *crisis decisions* in the Western sense.

Western evangelists often aim to bring an individual to a logical, emotion-laden decision. This individualistic decision-making, while relevant to some democratic, educated cultures, is foreign to Scripture. It fails to build strong churches in most cultures; those who "decide for Christ" this way usually do not follow through. A better illustration of entering the Christian life is that of emigrating from one Kingdom to a new one. The consequences of the move need to be weighed and would normally be discussed at length by the whole family.

Patterson reports the following experience with Western-style evangelism in Honduras:

We began witnessing with the usual American

emphasis, without lasting results. Several evangelists who were effective in the United States held campaigns during our first years of work in Honduras, and we helped them set up their meetings. But their methods proved ineffective in Honduras, in terms of converts followed through. This forced us to look again in Scripture at what the gospel was and how the apostles presented it. We did not find the Western emphasis on individual, crisis decisions. We found a greater emphasis on the resurrection, on repentance, and on bringing entire families as units to the Lord than what we were used to.

68. Do not count converts until they are added to a church, by baptism, that obeys the Lord's basic commands in love.

We should be leery of counting heads as new "Kingdom people" before they do the three things taken for granted by the apostles in Acts 2:38-41: Repent of their sins, be baptized, and be added to (identified with) the people of God. This is the pattern commanded by Peter in answer to the question that faith begs, "Brethren, what shall we do?" (Acts 2:37). These three activities in themselves do not save people but rather are the ratifying actions of the faith by means of which God saves us in Christ.

69. Start with the *basic stories of redemption.*

Give preference to Bible stories about the gospel and the basic truths of the holiness of the supremely powerful God, which the people can begin at once repeating to their family and friends. In most cultures, heads of households and "persons of peace" will repeat these stories, provided we tell them in a way they can imitate. Do not start with a philosophical or theological approach to the gospels--that comes later. Such oral communication of the gospel, including stories of conversions and healings, is normally the cutting edge of people movements for Christ.

70. Help *unconverted* heads of households and other natural leaders to communicate the gospel to their own families or friends, even before they are saved.

Use methods of witnessing that they can immediately imitate. They cannot imitate us if we draw on our experience and theological training to talk.

71. Get everyone to *talking about the gospel* on the streets, in the bars, at work--everywhere.

72. Use methods that are *easily imitated* at once by those we train.

Few Christians come to Christ or even form their most basic beliefs through the written page or from pulpit sermons. Nearly always, the Spirit of God uses other people. To verify effective witnessing methods, find what results have been obtained by others in the area, or in other fields with a similar culture and educational level. Remember: telling Bible stories enables a people movement to spread. Church planters should have stories ready that present each vital Christian truth and each essential area of the Christian life.

73. Use the *Old Testament,* too.

The more distant a culture is from the Christian worldview, the more Old Testament stories we need to tell to prepare the people to understand redemption. Old Testament stories enable potential converts to grasp the truths of one holy and all-powerful God who punishes sin, God's election of his own people, covenants between God and human beings, faith, sacrifice for sin, servant leadership, prayer, intercession, God's dealing with people in blocs (he sees people in solidarity, united as one in marriage, extended families, nations, and the whole human race in Adam). We relate a story from the Old Testament to introduce a concept in its earthly form (such as the need for a sacrifice for sin, as in the account of Cain and Abel in Gen. 4). Later we add a story from the New Testament to give the spiritual application. Other religions (Buddhism, Hinduism, New Age, Mormonism, Jehovah's Witnesses, etc.) begin with a philosophical view of God and religion, then add historical accounts to support or illustrate it. But the Old Testament prophets and New Testament apostles related the historical facts first, then built their philosophical doctrine on them. Both the old and new covenants start with great redemptive, historical facts.

The great redemptive-historical events are easy and interesting to relate to the average person in a non-Christian society. They include the fall of Adam; the flood; the covenant with Abraham; the miraculous escape from slavery in Egypt; the giving of the law; the establishment, division, and fall of the Kingdom; the exile and restoration; the birth of the Messiah; and his baptism, temptation, teaching, miracles, transfiguration, arrest, trial, death, resurrection, and ascension. The Psalms, Prophets, and Epistles explain how these historical facts bear on us. So we first tell the stories; later we add the doctrinal commentaries about them, as in the Epistles.

74. Follow up conversion with baptism as soon as possible.

The apostles gave extended instruction *after* baptism. An evangelist's job is done only when a convert is baptized and obeying the commands of Jesus. As seen in Peter's actions in Acts 2 as well as all other examples from the book of Acts, an evangelist's duty is not only to witness about Jesus Christ. Peter did not consider his work done until the converts had decided to turn away from a life of unrighteousness (repented), confirmed their commitment to follow the Savior with baptism, and were added to a body where they learned the patterns of the new Kingdom they had entered. "Belief" that merely acknowledges the facts is a poor criterion to distinguish those in the Kingdom from others outside. Heartfelt belief in Christ and Scripture is always accompanied by works because it includes the regenerating work of the Holy Spirit, as demonstrated in Acts 2:37-47. Some churches require a doctrinal course for baptism that automatically excludes illiterates; this makes baptism into a kind of graduation ceremony: something foreign to Scripture.

New converts should also begin celebrating the Lord's Supper as soon as possible, even though you have only one, two, or three converts in a new church in a pioneer field. Saving faith results in good works--at least an initial attempt at obedience. Make sure the converts do not confuse the cause and the result (a convert obeys because he or she has been saved; salvation does not come because of obedience). We can expect growth--not perfection--in obedience from the beginning. But a convert should obey out of love for Jesus, not out of a legalistic sense of duty (John 14:15).

75. Assure each convert of the church's loving acceptance at once.

Converts find it easy to obey Jesus when they know that he loves them; and they believe this when his body (the church) shows love for them. We also assure them immediately of the Holy Spirit's regeneration, sealing, and presence in their life. We do not mean a course of systematic doctrine about the Holy Spirit at this time. Physically embracing the convert immediately after baptism will be more assuring at this stage, with simple words to the effect, "You are risen with Jesus for all eternity, by the power of God's Spirit in you!" Some pastors lay hands on new converts when they baptize them, as the apostles did in Samaria, as a physical sign and assurance of having received the Holy Spirit (Acts 8:14-17).

We should deny full acceptance into the body until the convert has repented, been baptized, and been added to the assembly by the evident work of the Holy Spirit. This protects the assembly from "rice Christians," who are like ticks on a dog--parasites on the body of Christ. Left unprotected, both ticks and dog die, which is good for neither. True believers, however, need to be included as soon as possible, lest they die like abandoned babies in a hostile world. (Scoggins's experience, as well as Patterson's, is that people can be added in a matter of days when properly evangelized and mentored.)

76. **Implementation:** Mark items in *Appendix E* that you will deal with later. Add specific plans to your ARF for pre-Christians; note general plans below:

_____

_____

_____

_____

_____

_____

10. The Viewpoint of the Evangelist

Recommended Bible Study: Acts 9:10-27. Look for several things that were done after his conversion, to bring the convert into full fellowship in the body of Christ.

Scoggins relates:

We use John 9 to explain the power and cost of a personal witness. We try to encourage people to write out their testimony in such a way that they can share it in a minute or two. I remember shortly after I came to Christ I was encouraged to do this. It was pointed out to me that Paul shared all or part of his testimony many times in his letters. After I did so, I shared it probably 100 times in the next year. And this from a recluse who insisted he would never share his faith!

77. Aim at more than mere *decisions*.

Remember, evangelism is not complete until converts have repented from a life of sin, been baptized, and been added to an assembly where they learn the new patterns of life consistent with the new Spirit who now dwells in them. At least one worker on a church planting team or in a small group must be using the spiritual gift of evangelism. The gift of evangelism is evidenced only when people do in fact turn from their sin to follow Jesus, in repentant faith. Also, the gift of evangelism, like all other spiritual gifts, is to be used in harmony with the use of the other gifts given to the body of Christ (Eph. 4:11-16).

An evangelist working independently from the churches contributes little to church planting and may do more harm than good in a pioneer field. They often push people to make decisions, then leave them without pastoral care. They are like a farmer who scatters wheat seed recklessly on a mountain side and then comes back years later looking for a harvest. For church reproduction, such irresponsible evangelism does more harm than good. It tends to be self-centered rather than God-centered. Often Jesus is presented as a ticket to heaven, or simply as an answer to all of a persons' problems. In either case, it places Jesus at our disposal and for our use. He becomes

If we're saved by faith then a simple decision is enough, right?

No.
We also repent and trust Jesus to forgive us.

Merely deciding to believe is a "cultural faith"-- like a Buddhist's.

a servant of man, rather than man a servant of God. This kind of self-centered evangelism often inoculates a people against the kind of dynamic discipling that Jesus commands and that results in a Spirit-led movement for Christ among them. In contrast, the evangelistic messages in the book of Acts proclaimed Jesus as both Lord (master or king) and Christ (savior or deliverer). Evangelism was

God's command to leave the things of this world and follow him in his Kingdom. Today, God-centered evangelism in a self-centered Western world will call people to change loyalties, from serving themselves to serving the living God (see 2 Cor. 5:14; Gal. 5:13).

78. If working with a cross-cultural church planting team, give preference to unevangelized fields.

The apostle Paul sought to evangelize where Jesus had not been preached, where he would not build on another man's foundation (Rom. 15:20-22). Jesus requires that some of his apostles ("sent ones," or missionaries) seek fields that are still neglected; we are to go to all nations (Matt. 28:19; John 4:35; 2 Cor. 10:15-16).

To target a specific people group (the original meaning of the word "nations" in Matt. 28:19), you may need to help your church to see that God wants us to focus on different people groups--not just nations in the strictly political sense. China, for example, is a cluster of hundreds of people groups, or nations in the biblical sense. For an example of this discernment of peoples, see Peter and Paul's distinction of fields of responsibility in Galatians 2:7-9.

79. Help those with the gift of evangelism to imitate the apostles' emphasis in their message, and to use the *keys*.

<u>Recommended Bible Story: Acts 3-4.</u> Look for how the apostles witnessed with power.

Effective cross-cultural evangelism by Westerners normally requires reworking our gospel message. The one essential gospel message is the death and resurrection of the Son of God, the eternal forgiveness of sins for whoever repents and believes in him, and our entrance into the new kingdom (a new, eternal, loving society of believers filled with the Spirit of God). We must not export our Western individualistic approach to witnessing, which is often unbalanced when compared to the apostles' witness. The apostles, for example, emphasized the resurrection more than most modern Western preachers do. Throughout the book of Acts it was the "punch line" of their witness. Jesus died for our sins but was risen to give us life. The same emphasis appears in the Epistles. The historical fact that God raised Jesus from the dead and promises to raise us in him is today also the powerful, triumphant event, the supremely good news, which the Holy Spirit uses to convert those who are convicted of their sin.

Westerners, sometimes armed with a neat and logical "plan of salvation," often emphasize almost exclusively the legal value of Jesus' death to provide our forgiveness from sin, to the neglect of his vicarious resurrection. We are risen in him the same way that we die in him. His resurrection is the vehicle of our salvation. Our participation in it is the only means of receiving eternal life (e.g., 1 Cor. 15). And we receive this life together with, and united with, others; Ephesians 2 and 3 vividly picture and explain this corporate dimension of our salvation.

A Westerner's witness often emphasizes Anselm's theory of the atonement and neglects other vital aspects of the gospel. This ancient definition of the atonement focuses correctly on the substitutionary aspect of the death of Jesus (he died in our place). As sometimes explained, however, it overlooks Jesus' resurrection as an essential part of his redemptive work. Scripture shows that we are mortal (Gen. 2:17; 3:4; 1 Cor. 15:53-54; 1 Tim. 6:16) and that we take on Christ's immortality by being risen in him (1 Cor. 15:12-28, 42-57; John 5:24-29; 11:23-26; 1 Peter 3:21; Rom. 8:11; Eph. 1:18-2:7; and others).

A Westerner's unbalanced message of evangelism often dwells on the facts surrounding Christ's death and the consequent justification of the sinner (Rom. 5) and hardly prepares the convert for the new, regenerate life he or she will live (Rom. 6-8). Salvation should result in spiritual and emotional healing. Some might debate whether the total (including physical) healing promised as part of Jesus' redemption takes place before our resurrection, but there is no debate over the fact that Jesus was raised to give us new life, starting now. Too often evangelists proclaim correctly that by Jesus' death sinners are justified but then they leave them impotent in terms of practicing righteousness, heirs of a "half-way" salvation that is irrelevant for a practical Christian life. Balanced evangelism includes regeneration as well as justification, leading into Kingdom living and continual spiritual healing. For this and other reasons related to culture, the typical Western style of witnessing is often ineffective. It certainly will be with the people of the remaining unreached fields and will impede church multiplication.

Use the "keys" for anointed witnessing. Tap the power of the Holy Spirit, who anoints us to witness for Christ (Acts 1:8). This power to witness includes authority to bind or loose, which refers to the "keys to the kingdom" promised first to Peter and later given to all his disciples (Matt. 16:16-19; 18:18). The "binding and loosing" mentioned in these passages refer to Christ's building his church through his witnesses, a process of "invasion." In Matthew 16 the power to bind and loose is for the church to invade the kingdom of this world (the "gates of hell" will not withstand it). In Matthew 18 it is to keep the kingdom of this world from invading the Kingdom of heaven, the church (see also 1 Cor. 5). In both cases God authorizes his church to act on earth in Jesus' all-powerful name, in the power and with the guidance of the Holy Spirit.

Some theologians would limit this power of the keys to the twelve Apostles; others include the bishops who succeeded them. But most agree, and this may be reassuring to you, that any true believer uses these keys--the power to bind or loose sins--as he witnesses to an unsaved person (or corrects a disorderly Christian) in the power of the Holy Spirit and in the all-powerful name of Jesus.

What is the power of the Holy Spirit to witness? Is it our courage or our shouting? Hardly. It is the anointing by God's Spirit on us and our testimony, as we declare a person's forgiveness in Jesus. We trust God to convince a sinner, by his Spirit, to repent and believe through our faithful testimony. The Holy Spirit glorifies Jesus in the heart of new believers, not only by convincing them subjectively of sin and the need for salvation, but also by loosing (forgiving) their sin before the Most Holy One. God's conversion of a sinner often depends more on the faith of the witness than on that of the convert. For example, the paralytic lowered through the roof to be healed by Jesus was first saved from his sins because of the faith of his friends (Mark 2:1-12; see also Acts 16:31).

More educated people often find it harder to witness this way, to believe for people who are still unable to believe for themselves. Third world Christians, for example, generally witness more fervently than Americans. Westerners tend to rely more on the logic and accuracy of their witness, rather than on God's power to convey Jesus' forgiveness and life.

Using the keys is always in connection with the church. Jesus made that clear. An independent Christian doing his or her own thing, with no accountability to God's leaders in the church, has a rather shaky claim on this authority to bind or loose.

80. Enable newly converted heads of families to lead weekly or bi-weekly "gathering meetings" for unbelievers.

In some cultures you can ask an adult male convert to invite friends--no Christians--to a low key Bible study or care group. Lead the study in such a way that he can imitate you at once, then let him take it over after a meeting or two and coach him from behind the scenes. When others are ready to convert, bring them into a group led by a more experienced believer or evangelist.

81. Where authorities, employers, friends or families are hostile against conversion to Christ, *allow converts to make their own decisions as to how they will testify.*

Let the converts decide if they want to be baptized publicly or in private (as the Ethiopian eunuch and the Philippian jailer were in Acts 8 and 16). It is their life and jobs that are in jeopardy, not ours, so we let them make the decision. In very hostile areas they may also decide to meet underground, forming clusters of tiny house churches rather than larger, Western style congregations. They may also decide to continue going to a Mosque to pray, just as Paul continued to go to the Jewish synagogues after his conversion. Again, this should be their decision; we allow the Holy Spirit to speak to them the same way that we expect him to lead us.

82. Implementation: Mark items by their number in Appendix E. Also, note your general plan to do the work of an evangelist (add them to your ARF's, too):

_____
_____
_____
_____
_____
_____
_____
_____

11. The Viewpoint of the
Church Multiplication Team

Why teams?

An *individual* like me needs freedom. I see things from a different point of view than you!

<u>**Recommended Bible Study: Mark 3:13-15; Acts 10:23-24; 13:1-3**</u>. Look for several things that Jesus or his apostles did to form teams.

Jesus and his apostles never traveled alone; they always worked as a team. Patterson relates how he discovered the value of this:

We began work in Latin America with the usual Western attitude of individualism. We did not think in terms of ministry teams. I had come to Jesus through an individual decision. I served with a mission agency that dealt with its missionaries on an individual basis. I stumbled in my individual way for several years before I learned from the Hondurans how easy it was to penetrate a neighborhood with the gospel if we worked as a team. It came natural for the Hondurans--when I kept out of their way.

Since working in Honduras I have been impressed

with the importance of sending *church based teams* (as in Acts 13:1-3). This does not bypass the mission agency, but places the responsibility of sending missionaries on the church rather than an agency. It can get local sending churches more involved, make it easier to raise support, provide better accountability, assure a more balanced distribution of spiritual gifts on the tea and avoid many of the problems that lead to missionary "burnout."

83. If you lead a team starting a new church or group, prepare an Activity Review File for *a new church or group* to follow.

You may need another ARF (besides the team's ARF) for the church or group to follow, led by their own local leaders. An example of a new church's ARF is given in *Appendix B*. Start listing activities, as Jesus commands in Matthew 28:18-20, with his basic commands. Key activities for a church multiplication team are listed in Appendix C.

If you don't have *Jesus' commands* memorized yet, they are:

Repent, believe, and receive the Holy Spirit;
Be baptized;
Celebrate the Lord's Supper;
Love God and one's neighbor in a practical way; forgive;
Pray;
Give;
Disciple others (witness, teach, remain in his Word).

Add other activities as you go along. Include those

ministries that grow out of Jesus' commands (these are expanded in chapter 17 on *The Church Leader*).

Patterson, after coaching several teams working in Asia and North Africa, observed, "Most of the teams that were failing had become ingrown. They knew what the team should do, but they had not listed the activities their converts or new churches would do. They could not *lead* the potential national leaders, because they had no clear vision of where they were going--so they only *taught* them. Some teams make the fatal mistake of pulling potential leaders out of the new churches to serve on the church planting *team*. They forget that the team is merely scaffolding. The scaffolding grows bigger and bigger; when someone starts working on the building itself, they pull him off and make him work on the scaffolding--sometimes in the name of *team spirit*!"

84. Imitate the outreach and witness of the apostles' church planting teams.

Recommended Bible Story: Acts 10:1-11:18. Look for church planting principles in this passage.

> What first prompted God to move? (What had both Cornelius and Peter been doing?)
>
> What did the mother church in Joppa do? (How was a *church-based* team involved?)
>
> How did God curb Peter's cultural prejudice?
>
> Who was invited to the *exclusive* meeting in Caesarea, apart from Peter and his companions?
>
> What kind of person was the contact Cornelius? What reputation had he with relatives and friends?
>
> What was the content of the witnesses' message?
>
> What did they do to confirm converts' salvation?
>
> How much time was spent with them?
>
> How did Peter deal with the grandmother church's objections to his cross-cultural approach?

Peter took other brothers in Christ from Joppa when they planted the new church in Cornelius's house in Caesarea (Acts 10:23). As always, they presented the *bare essentials of the gospel* (Acts 10:36-43):

> *Who Jesus is*: Lord of all, anointed by God to do good and heal (10:36-38);
>
> *His death for forgiveness of sins* (10:39);
>
> *His resurrection from the dead* (10:40-42);

Our response: *faith* (10:43)

85. Eliminate a major cause of missionary failure and burnout by deploying *church-based teams*.

As we know, Jesus and his apostles did not work alone; they formed apostolic bands (Mark 3:13-15; Acts 10:23-24; 13:1-3). Jesus' command to "go" in the Great Commission was collective, for the church. He did not mean for it to take on the modern individualistic approach, which owes its origin to Western culture rather than the New Testament. The apostolic bands that accompanied Peter and Paul were midwives that enabled mother churches to reproduce daughter churches--a function of the body of Christ, not of individuals.

Church planters work better together, combining the spiritual gifts of several persons. For example, the Holy Spirit works far more powerfully though a group of four than through four persons working alone. The church is repeatedly represented in Scripture as an active army or united body--not as a school or a collection of individual Christians.

By forming a church-based team, we do not mean joining an existing "team" already put together on a field by a mission agency for administrative convenience. The missionaries' home church (often in cooperation with sister churches) forms the team as an extension of its own body life and out of love for the missionaries. They might send an entire team through a mission agency, rather than individuals or couples. More churches are seeing the need for a church-based team effort as opposed to the modern tradition of going to the mission field on an individual or single family basis. Churches that form apostolic teams take responsibility for their support and hold them accountable to reproduce new churches. The church itself is a reproducing body (Eph. 4.16)--a team. Thus, in the New Testament living bodies (churches) reproduced themselves in living bodies (daughter churches) through the instrumentality of living bodies (church planting teams).

86. To avoid tensions in the home, help married church planters to *define the wife's role in ministry*.

A married couple must agree on what the wife does in the church-related ministry. Frequently stress grows out of misunderstandings about what she should do. They discuss it openly and frankly. A husband and wife have distinctly different roles in fulfilling the call of God upon their lives. These roles vary as their circumstances change. For instance, if a couple goes to the field with no children, they may both be heavily involved in language learning, evangelism, and so forth. A couple arriving with young children, however, find that someone must take care of the children. In God's order for the family this falls to the mother (Titus 2:3-5). She will be less involved in certain church activities than her husband. This is no problem--unless she feels that her calling is less important before God than her husband's.

Missionary couples, especially from the West, where the difference between the sexes tend to be denied, sometimes fail, with disastrous results, to recognize the inherent differences between men and women and their God-given roles in marriage. They often need help to live out God's calling for their lives rather than the expectations of their college professors, friends, or misguided spouse.

Note that a woman, Priscilla, helped disciple Apollos on the leadership level, presumably under her husband's or Paul's authority (Acts 18:1-4). Also, Philip's daughters prophesied (Acts 21:8-9). Thus we see that scriptural admonitions against women's teaching men or exercising leadership in the church are not absolute prohibitions. God enabled women to lead under male authority.

87. If you are a team leader, help your members to *agree that the church multiplication team is temporary* in a locale.

The team normally phases out as local "inside" or national leaders begin helping their own churches to multiply. Do not let your church planting team become an end in itself. Remember, its members are midwives, temporary scaffolding, to enable their sending church(es) to reproduce. If no "mother" church exists yet within the target culture, it should be formed as soon as possible. (At first it might have as few as two or three converts.) Remember, team members from outside the culture must not outnumber converts in meetings during the formative stages of a church. Some team members may need to be absent during key services in the beginning. The newborn church must sense its identify within the culture, or converts feel they are joining a group of outsiders and the church takes on an "outsider" mentality that cannot reproduce within the culture.

88. Before joining a team, *determine prayerfully with whom you should work.*

Trust your life's career only to a team leader who wholeheartedly encourages you to minister in a way for which you are gifted and to which God has called you. Serve with people, teams, churches, or mission agencies that put loving, childlike obedience to Christ ahead of all other policies, including their own. Join an existing team or organization only if its leadership (especially your potential field supervisor or team leader) assures you that your gifts and ministry are needed, wanted, and apt to be productive. Make sure you won't be shunted into a ministry for which God has not gifted you, which often happens in Christian organizations. Avoid leaders who, for the sake of conformity--often mistakenly called "unity"--force you to conform to human rules or policies. True unity in Christ brings out our differences and frees us for distinct ministries in the united body (1 Cor. 12).

89. *Appreciate the differences in another culture,* especially if you are entering a pioneer field.

God loves the distinctive features of different races and cultures. He created the nations; every tribe, tongue, and people group will be present in glory--with their wonderful cultural differences (Rev. 7:9). We violate God's plan when we force cultures to integrate in the name of Christian unity. When we force two cultures to combine in one church, they never *integrate*: the stronger culture, the one with more money and political power, cancels out the weaker, even though the stronger may have fewer people. True unity in Christ retains cultural differences in loving harmony with each other (sister churches with different customs love one another and cooperate in God's work). To try to integrate two cultures does not unify them; it brings about the death of one of the cultures, of something that God loves dearly.

90. Investigate carefully a potential target field and the best way to penetrate it.

Before planning in detail how to reach a culturally distant people group, we discern its main culture and subcultures and recruit witnesses and church planters from the same class of people or a similar culture (match church planters with people of a similar culture).

The first question to ask about an unreached people group is, *Who can best reach them*? As a general rule, the most effective witness comes from those who are culturally close to the people of the targeted community. It is often wiser to mobilize church planters from churches of the third world than for Americans or Europeans to do it alone, especially for the initial penetration when evangelism has to be done by outsiders.

91. Focus on one specific people group and subculture.

For effective church reproduction we target a single *homogeneous* unit (i.e., the largest number of people among whom the gospel can spread without being hindered by class or cultural differences). It is virtually impossible to plant a national church that reproduces spontaneously in a pioneer field without focusing on a specific class of people. When converts are outnumbered by people of another economic level, social class, or subculture, they fail to sense that the church is being born with their own cultural identity.

In a pioneer field the most responsive people are normally of the working class, but not necessarily the poorest. For example, the apostle Paul often targeted the disenfranchised middle class--an economic group of hard-working folk who had been successful economically but who would never be able to rise to a commensurate status (e.g., freed slaves such as Onesimus, merchants of non-aristocratic birth such as Lydia, or exiled Jewish merchants such as Aquilla and Priscilla). These frustrated workers are usually open to a new avenue of change, even if it is ''counter-cultural.''

92. Arrange on-the-job training, if needed, for team members from another country or ethnic group.

Nationals from another country or race who join your team nearly always need help to gear their methods of communication to the target community, even though they come from a culturally close people. If you mobilize workers from another country for a team who are culturally closer to the target field, they will still need cross-cultural training, even when the cultural differ-

ence is slight. Their training may also include vocational training, for skills needed for self-employment or small business, especially for fields of restricted access. Remember, we do not expect outsiders, even if they are culturally closer than we are, to reproduce churches. The impulse for spontaneous multiplication is given by the Holy Spirit to the local people. All outside church planting team members must learn to disciple from behind the scenes.

93. Target a responsive segment of the population.

Jesus sent his apostles to people who responded to the gospel. He warned them to ''shake the dust off their feet'' as a sign of Gods judgment against those that did not heed it (Luke 10:4-16). Some missionaries waste unfortunate years of ministry on people whom God has not chosen for salvation, neglecting others close by who are ready. Often this becomes evident when missionaries shift their aim to another people and see, in a few months, more fruit than they saw in many years among the first people.

94. Help national leaders to take full pastoral responsibility as soon as possible.

But things will grow out of my control !

That's what we want!

As soon as you start training a pastor/elder, start giving him more and more pastoral responsibility. A church seldom reproduces if it depends on outside control or subsidy. For the Holy Spirit to move local leaders to multiply daughter churches, they must take the initiative in freedom. Most if not all of new pastors/elders training in a pioneer field should be trained on the job to assure church multiplication; leaders trained in traditional, classroom-only institutions seldom think in terms of church growth by reproduction.

95. Once churches are multiplying, *avoid burnout* by turning over problems to the new elders, and moving to new areas.

As churches start to multiply, more and more pressure is put on the original team leader to deal with stressful situations in the churches. All effective church planters experience this stress. Paul agonized over the problems in the infant churches in Galatia: "My dear children, for whom I am again in the pains of childbirth . . ." (Gal. 4:19). After listing many perils and painful adventures experienced in his church planting work, he added, "Besides everything else, I face daily the pressure of my concern for all the churches. Who is weak, and I do not feel weak? Who is led into sin, and I do not inwardly burn?" (2 Cor. 11:28-29).

When churches begin to multiply, we discipline ourselves to turn over stressful problems to others with the pastoral gift. In line with the advice Jethro gave to Moses, when we first feel the pressures accumulating, we put distance between ourselves and the people in the congregations. This forces the newer elders to share more in problem-solving. We are more experienced to deal with pastoral-type problems, and they would be foolish not to come to us with the tougher ones. But we must let them make more mistakes. We must be less available. We make more thorough use of what Paul called the "presbytery" (1 Tim. 4:14, the group of elders that oversee as a body the work of the churches). Do not let an elder tackle a really stressful problem as an individual; show him how to deal with it as a corporate body of elders.

Patterson mentions how he learned to deal with the ever-increasing stressful situations:

In Honduras, where we did not have enough really mature pastors or elders in a certain area to handle a painful church situation, we created temporary committee of elders. These committees consisted of as many elders or pastors from as many churches as we could get to meet together at the location of the problem; we occasionally asked elders/pastors from other churches not of our own fellowship. They studied the case, interviewed the persons involved, then gave to the local church their recommendation (which was virtually always followed). I made it a point not to be present at these meetings, although I often helped arrange them.

Even so, workers continued to come to me with too many serious problems. To protect my health and my family, I had to put physical distance between myself and the churches. I started to have more short vacations with my family. Once we moved to a whole new area and began to start new clusters of churches quite separate from the first churches. This lessened the strain considerably; the elders saw much less of me and took on far more responsibility. You could almost see them maturing. They stopped accusing me of neglecting the churches because they respected the fact that I was starting new churches.

Also, to safeguard my sanity, I disciplined myself to keep turning over all the churches (with their problems) to God in prayer. I had to become more willing to trust him, against all human odds, to bring the church through their birth and adolescent pains. Often I prayed, for the sake of my own mental health as well as for the churches, "Lord, they're your churches, not mine. If they depend on me, then let them fail! If you want them to keep growing and reproducing, only you can do the work of grace needed to overcome their problems. I am willing to let them fail. I disown any claim to ownership. They are yours. Simply use me as an instrument to do your will." Many times I had to rededicate myself to teach simply and to practice loving obedience to Jesus' commands, and then I left the rest to God, trusting him to help the new elders, inexperienced as they were, to deal with the problems. I also asked my wife to keep my time schedule for me and to ration the time I spent with stressful problems; that forced me to delegate (and pray) more!

Yes, some churches--a very few compared to the total--did fail when we gave them less attention. These were the chronic complainers, the churches that seemed to enjoy their own problems and the attention we gave them. Analyzing them with our Bibles open, God soon gave us the assurance that new churches that remain dependent on outsiders' help deserve to fail. They are parasites on the body of Christ--sponges that keep absorbing pastoral care and seldom develop outgoing pastoral work or spiritual effort of their own. A person with the pastoral gift may want to continue shepherding such churches, but an apostle called to be a cross-cultural church planter should shake the dust off his feet as soon as he detects this abnormal lack of discipleship.

God knows better than anyone that the main church planter lacks time to deal with (or even worry about) all the problems that new churches will have. That is why Paul told Titus to establish elders in all the churches so that he could turn over the pastoral work to them. Those things that you don't have time to do or that you would have to neglect your family in trying to do or that would burn yourself out physically or mentally trying to do are not God's will for you.

96. Recruit team members committed to seeing the job through.

They commit simply to do what Jesus says: to disciple a people group, no matter how long it takes or what sacrifice is required. If your church has "adopted" an unreached people group and is praying for it, God will raise up people with the apostolic gift that your church can send to disciple. If your church is small, it can cooperate with sister churches to put together an apostolic team. For cross-cultural church reproduction, especially in difficult pioneer fields, a career commitment is essential for church multiplication. For this apostolic gift and calling, God honors the commitment to do just as he says: disciple a people--not to stay a certain number of years. Short-term commitments to serve in distant fields are valid to gain exposure to a foreign field to test one's gifts and discern God's call or to gain experience to serve better in the home church. But short-term work in another culture does not result in church reproduction. A list of *Practical Helps for Selecting Team Members who Meet the Requirements of a Specific Field and Ministry* is given at the end of this chapter.

97. Filter out non-essentials.

Discern and lay aside all nontransferable methods, attitudes, and equipment--including the way we teach or preach and our style of worship. Do nothing in the new culture that is not easy to imitate and be passed on at once. Patterson relates how he brought this filtering process to church planting teams in Asia:

I asked them what kind of churches would take root among the people, in their own culture, and reproduce in even the poorest slums and most remote villages. They started to answer theologically so I asked them if these churches would start with the people sitting on benches as we were doing. They said no, that the churches would start in very poor homes and they would sit on the floor. So we moved the benches back and sat on the floor for our workshop and worship. We also took off our shoes and the women sat to one side, just as they would do in a culturally relevant church. We also filtered out Western music. I had them take ten minutes to compose a praise song from a line in the Psalms, and sing it in their own musical style--no Western sound! The cook, a neighbor and a friend came running into the room, happily surprised, to hear praises sung in their own style!

Methods for training pastors in pioneer fields are often painfully irrelevant to their culture. Training by outsiders or by institutions receiving outside help, rather than by more-experienced pastors or elders in the churches themselves, often stifles the spontaneous reproduction of national churches.

To filter out irrelevant methods as we cross into another culture, we discern between two large blocs of unreached peoples:

1. Those in *open* fields--where church planters can work legally;

2. Those in fields of *restricted access*--where church planters work underground, as literal outlaws (here our methods must be radically different; we filter out far more Western traditions).

What we screen out becomes obvious if we let the Word of God be our filter. This becomes confused if our criteria for filtering come mainly from anthropological studies. The greater the cultural difference or the more restricted the field, the more careful we are to filter out what is not explicitly commanded in the New Testament.

98. Select team members who meet the requirements of your specific field and ministry.

Look for persons who:

- ☐ come from the same mother church, or like-minded sister churches (i.e., they already know each other and work well together);

- ☐ are willing to work bi-vocationally when necessary (especially if working in very poor fields or in fields of restricted access);

- ☐ are heartily recommended by those who know them well and who pray continually for them in their home church (good ministry grows out of good relationships);

- ☐ are called by God to serve as career church planters (church multiplication requires workers committed to disciple the people as Jesus says-- not short-term visitors or those who simply use a church planting effort to launch another ministry);

- ☐ readily bond in love with the people of a new culture;

- ☐ submit willingly to the team leader or auxiliary leader if leadership is shared;

- ☐ agree on objectives and methods;

- ☐ agree on basic doctrinal beliefs and church practices;

- ☐ share similar social, economic, and educational backgrounds;

- ☐ receive ongoing training and evaluation;

- ☐ can disciple and delegate responsibility to new local leaders;

- ☐ know how to wage spiritual warfare against demonic powers (the ultimate battle is not against culture, Islam, or atheism, but against Satan and his demons, who only use culture: Eph. 6:11-13).

- ☐ have a cross-bearing disciple's commitment (are willing to give their life, if necessary, to extend the Kingdom of God among their chosen people: Luke 9:23-24).

99. Plan the *essential activities* for a church multiplication team.

Ask the Lord to help you see what your churches will be doing in the future. Appendix C also expands on these same activities, if you need help. If you lead or supervise a church planting team, you will find your job easier if your team's *Activity Review File* includes these activities for team members:

Prayerfully select and focus on the specific people you plan to disciple.

Target people who are culturally similar to you and your team members.

Bond with those you have chosen.

Bind Satan.

Maintain constant, fervent prayer for the unsaved and for converts.

Seek good contacts.

Witness for Jesus.

Baptize. Baptize entire families as soon as possible, as the apostles did.

Break bread.

Teach.

Organize.

Agree on each leader's wife's ministry (on the team and among the new pastors/elders).

Keep doing evangelism in the community--especially after starting public worship services.

Make worship an edifying celebration.

Give responsibility to the local leaders and avoid overcontrol or subsidizing by outsiders.

Arrange for clear, regular accountability for everybody.

100. **Implementation: See Appendix C, *An Example of an ARF for a Church Multiplication Team.*** It includes detailed lists of activities for:

> *Starting* a new church.

> *Organizing* for church multiplication.

> *Managing one's time* for church multiplication.

> *A separation ceremony* for the team.

> *8 categories of people* to mobilize on the field.

> Also, mark applicable items by their numbers in *Appendix E.*

> And, add plans to your ARFs to mobilize church planting teams.

Please note your general plans now:

_____

_____

_____

_____

_____

_____

_____

_____

_____

_____

12. The Viewpoint of the Field Supervisor

Recommended Bible Study: Matthew 20:20-28 (see also 1 Peter 5:1-4). Look for the correct attitudes of a good leader in the Kingdom of God.

Patterson relates the advantage of having a good field supervisor:

During my first term on the field we served under Virgil Gerber, a rare field supervisor who knew what discipling was. He was the first person I heard use the word "disciple" as a verb. And he applied it to training pastors! He made me set goals and plan the small steps to reach them. He told us to stop training pastors in our traditional way, when it didn't produce results. At first I felt a bit hostile toward him, but God used Virgil to start me thinking as a discipler and to appreciate a flexible, caring field supervisor.

101. Help those with the apostolic gift to select their field wisely.

A pioneer cross-cultural church planting team needs workers with the apostolic gift and calling to work where the gospel has not yet been proclaimed (Rom. 15:20-22). Help them to find the receptive people within the chosen field and to trust God to lead them to people whom he has already prepared, who have been chosen from before the foundation of the world to be saved (Eph. 1:4).

The most receptive social units are very often the ones most hidden. All fields have a wide variety of people groups or subcultures; the common workers and the ones who are oppressed almost always are the most receptive to the gospel but are also almost always the least conspicuous to a Western missionary. Jesus made a point of the fact that he came to proclaim the gospel to the poor. He began his public ministry among the working class in Galilee; had he begun in Jerusalem or some other nerve center with natural leaders, he would have been crucified prematurely.

Those of the upper or affluent, satisfied middle class who wield power seldom respond during the first generation of discipling. They normally resist change of the status quo. They will occasionally convert as individuals, especially among students, but they resist a grass-roots people movement for Christ. Seldom is a reproducing church started first among the middle class in a pioneer field.

When they first penetrate an unreached field, however,

American missionaries often target the middle class, with whom they most easily bond because of similar education or economic backgrounds. Do not assume that you can reach an unreached people group in a pioneer field from the top down, unless it is a small, closely knit tribe. This top-down approach works only with second- or third-generation Christians, as seen now in Latin America, Africa south of the Sahara, the Philippines, South Korea, and southern India. We discipline ourselves to detect the most responsive subcultures within a homogeneous unit. This subculture is often defined even more strongly by economic differences than racial.

Missionaries sometimes describe a people as hard when in fact the people would be quite receptive to Christ if he were presented in a more culturally relevant way. Church planters sometimes needlessly provoke a negative response by overreacting to, or prematurely attacking, idolatrous practices and other "sins" of the culture. Let us exercise at least as much patience as we expect others to have with the obvious shortcomings of our own evangelical subculture.

102. Take advantage of the brutal class discrimination in most resistant fields (but avoid messy foreign politics).

For the initial penetration of highly restricted areas, such as China and most of Asia, seek to live among people who want change, who do not defend the status quo. Also, seek to live where authorities do not watch closely.

103. Help team members to bond with their people.

Church planters should feel God's call to the specific people they are targeting and should be dedicated to carrying out their discipling as Jesus commanded (not simply to do some project among them). They need to live among them and appreciate their distinct ways; no matter how corrupt a culture may be, God has always planted beautiful things in it.

> **Add plans to your ARFs now to select your field, find the most receptive people in it, and bond with them and with the culture, if applicable.**

104. To keep everyone working in loving harmony, *personally disciple others just as Jesus commanded and modeled it.*

Truly biblical discipling requires that we do the following things:

- ✔ *Fish for men* (Matt. 4:19); witness to people who are lost (e.g., Jesus and Nicodemus, the Samaritan woman, the nations of Matt. 28:19).
- ✔ *Teach obedience to Christ's commands to all nations* (Matt. 28:19-20); penetrate unreached people groups and help them to reproduce their own obedient congregations among their own people—and among other unreached groups.

Do you remember Jesus' commands? Let us take one more chance to review them (nothing is more important):

> *Repent and believe, and be filled with the Spirit* (biblical repentance is an eternal change of our innermost will and being, to turn from sin to serve God);
>
> *Be baptized* (and continue in the new, holy life that it initiates);
>
> *Celebrate the Lord's Supper* (and maintain the holy communion with Christ and his body that it affirms);
>
> *Love* God and people (in a practical, forgiving way);
>
> *Pray*;
>
> *Give*;
>
> *Disciple others* (witness, teach the Word, train leaders).

- ✔ *Cooperate lovingly with fellow disciples.* Our love should be evident to all the world (John 13:34-35).
- ✔ *Make a total commitment.* Bear one's cross sacrificially--to one's death if needed--to carry out Jesus' commission (Luke 9:23). Patterson confesses,

> In seminary, I and some of my buddies suspected that this sacrificial discipleship mentality was a bit fanatical. We did not really want to practice or preach it. We sought position and security with an established church or mission agency. After my first convert in northern Honduras was hacked to death by machete following his baptism, I was forced to rethink seriously and painfully my whole commitment. God let me see

at that time that my security-minded attitude was stifling church reproduction. My measured commitment was contagious; other workers also began to seek position.

✔ *Train pastors and missionaries by personally discipling them* (as Jesus did for the twelve apostles, Paul for Timothy and Titus, Aquilla and Priscilla for Apollos).

Mobilizing local nationals for ministry gets top priority. The best way to assure a church's healthy birth is to train the local elders--soon. Remember to use their home as a classroom. Their wife and children will do a good job of exposing their flaws! Basic shepherding skills, including teaching, are used with the wife and children as well as basic lessons on discipline. The home is the best place to learn these lessons. Likewise, many a leader has been undone by failure in his own home. Use the congregation as a classroom as well. The team members train local leaders immediately to begin shepherding and discipling others, by personally discipling them. In most of the remaining unreached fields we must avoid "classroom only" teaching in which professors take little personal responsibility for the present, effective ministry of their students. In restricted fields, where growth comes from multiplying clusters of tiny home churches, a much larger number of pastors/elders are needed for the same amount of believers. Even new pastors/elders of tiny house churches must continually train their own "Timothies" to shepherd the daughter and granddaughter churches.

105. Disciple *new leaders in another culture* the way Jesus and his apostles modeled discipling.

Discipling on a pastoral level is characterized in the Bible by practicing loving obedience, maintaining an apprentice-type relationship between teacher and student (which involves lots of time spent together), relating the Word to a student's practical work, holding students accountable for practical pastoral ministry, modeling pastoral skills, and taking responsibility for the effectiveness of a student's present ministry. Personal discipling is not one-on-one tutoring. It may be with only one person, but tutoring per se is not its purpose. Jesus discipled twelve at the top leadership level. Paul always had a small apostolic band. Personal discipling is personal in that one takes personal responsibility for the discipline and effective ministry of each person in training. Thus the pastoral-level disciple meets regularly with his teacher to report his progress, plan his next activities, study the Word, and pray. Personal discipling also requires accompanying students in their field of work. Planting churches directly from a mission base or missionary compound is usually ineffective. Workers must live among the target people, bond with them, and work closely together with their potential leaders.

106. Launch a team for a distant field with a *serious separation ceremony.*

Separate the church planters through the power of the Holy Spirit, as in Acts 13:1-3. This assures them of the church's prayerful support, allows better accountability to the church, and gives the missionaries a greater sense of security and reassurance during hard times on the field. The church in Antioch separated Paul, Barnabas, and Mark to disciple the nations with much prayer and fasting. This must separate the workers for church planting in another field not only physically but also emotionally--from their home church, family, mission base, or friends.

Some organizations practice frequent laying on of hands for blessing and power for ministry. In this case, the separation ceremony may not be very meaningful if all you do is lay on hands again. You make it special, so that all involved know that the apostles ("sent ones") have truly been sent by the body through the power of God's Spirit. Perhaps that is why the church in Antioch fasted first (Acts 13:1-3).

107. Do *strategic planning*, to mobilize different types of people on the field.

If you are a leader, add plans to your ARFs to mobilize the following *categories of persons or groups* (mark those needing special attention):

☐ The new national church.

Envision a national church in a currently unreached field, obeying Jesus' commands and therefore reproducing--often in tiny house churches--among its own people (Matt. 28:18-20).

Wise mission planners, like military strategists, begin with long-range objectives stated so clearly that each preparatory step is self-evident. In planning for a specific unreached field, they keep its limited resources or freedom in mind and reason backward through preparatory steps, avoiding programs too expensive or too electronic for national churches to reproduce.

But first, we prepare the right kind of:

☐ Key national leaders.

For widespread church reproduction, new servant leaders on the regional (synod) level mobilize other pastors--a skill acquired from disciplers who take personal, loving responsibility for the fruitful ministry of others, otherwise they become grasping and demanding.

But first we develop the right kind of:

☐ National pastors/elders.

Good pastors mobilize others for ministry (Eph. 4:11-16)--a skill acquired on the job, not in classrooms.

But first we must properly train:

☐ Potential national leaders who are *servants, shepherds, and mobilizers.*

Pastoral students are not simply educated but are trained to edify and mobilize the local body of Christ (Eph. 4:11-16). In most fields, this happens best in churches where trainers harmonize their teaching with other gifts (1 Cor. 12-13). Remember: balanced discipling relates the Word to the work in love--teaching in love to mobilize our disciples to do God's work. In most pioneer fields formal institutional training is impractical. Elder types cannot leave their responsibilities. Economically motivated youths respond but, lacking preparatory education, cannot assimilate the intensive input and, lacking models of well-established churches, cannot realistically apply it.

But first we lay a discipleship foundation with:

☐ New Christians.

We teach believers before all else to obey Jesus' commands (Matt. 28:19-20)--believe, repent, be baptized and receive the Holy Spirit, love, break bread, pray, give, and disciple others (Acts 2:38-47). Prolonged indoctrination before loving obedience stifles the sacrificial discipleship and makes it harder to mobilize one for ministry. We help new believers to see themselves as highly disciplined pilgrims in search of a better country. The journey is difficult but exhilarating. What a privilege to labor in Jesus' Kingdom; what joy! We were created--and re-created--for this! We help brand new believers to find real joy in serving our King. This joy of serving is not reserved for some elite group in the Kingdom (e.g., full-time clergy). Every child of God is enlisted in God's army to wage warfare--and not as volunteers in an auxiliary branch of the army when they feel like it, leaving the "real work" to the clergy of the regular army. Even George Washington found that such an army could not win a war. When we are conscripted into this army, we find a whole new discipline; our whole life is changed.

But first we establish the type of relationship that loving discipling can build on, with:

☐ Pre-Christians.

We let the converts see the crucified and risen Christ living in us (2 Cor. 5:15)--the full, sacrificial, abundant, pilgrim life lived out in a hostile world. They see us modeling the loving relationships needed for further discipling and witnessing of Jesus' saving death and resurrection in a way they can imitate lovingly with their family and friends.

But first we form a church multiplication team skilled in properly discipling converts and leaders:

☐ The team entering the target field.

Teams, then, not only combine the needed gifts and cooperative spirit but screen out technology, equipment, and methods that nationals cannot imitate, afford, or pass on.

But first we may need to join with:

☐ Missionaries from the two-thirds world.

We might become partners with emerging churches that are now mobilizing their own foreign missionaries, who relate better to many unreached peoples. No amount of training to adapt to a new culture equals being born culturally close--that is, having similar politics, race, language, economic and education levels, family size, rural/urban life-style, and world view.

But first we may need to deal with:

☐ Bi-vocational missionaries.

Only bi-vocational missionaries can reside in most of the remaining unreached fields long enough for church multiplication. They need, like Paul, cross-cultural church planting experience, teams, formal commissioning (Acts 13:1-3), and employment such as a small business that puts them with the working class.

108. Help your workers evaluate their use of ministry time

Let us manage our limited time in a way that honors God. Reproductive evangelism and church multiplication take enormous amounts of time. To establish priorities daily and over the years, we keep in mind Jesus' explicit commands and our God-given priorities (Eph. 5.15-17).

Mark the *time management guidelines* that you or your coworkers should agree to follow:

☐ Delegate pastoral and evangelistic responsibilities to other leaders.

Let regular members do things; once someone agrees to do something, avoid overcontrol of his or her work. Do not use your wife (or husband) merely to run errands unless that is the role you both have agreed upon for her (or him).

☐ Give your family ample time each day, and a whole day (on the average) per week.

Take your Sabbaths (there was a time when you might have been stoned to death if you didn't)! Do not allow your family to feel that they have to compete for your time.

☐ Discuss your ministry regularly with your spouse and children so that they appreciate it and do not begrudge the time you spend away.

Talk and pray with them about your plans (and theirs) before you travel and review with them what happened (to them, too) when you return.

☐ Avoid arguing with skeptics.

New missionaries, looking earnestly for contacts, often cast their pearls before swine. We may enjoy an occasional friendly theological argument, but we must not get caught up in controversial issues. We discipline ourselves to avoid non-edifying details of theological discussions (remember Paul's warnings about foolish questions and genealogies; see 1 Tim. 1:4; Titus 3:9). Sometimes we cannot avoid a controversy. But we can avoid giving it too much time; keep doing the positive things you know God wants you to do. Don't feel you always have to prove yourself right. (It is dangerous for a human always to be right.)

☐ Start immediately turning over long-range leadership responsibilities to local leaders.

Train adults who are potential leaders; give them responsibilities as soon as they are ready.

☐ Keep analyzing how you spent your time during the day or previous week.

Be ruthless in cutting out of your agenda all activities--no matter how enjoyable--that do not move you measurably toward your God-given goals. Avoid too much television or other forms of entertainment that do not edify or unite your family.

☐ Have another person monitor your progress.

No one can effectively evaluate the use of his or her own time; we all need someone to help us.

☐ If you are a hard-working husband, you might have another person--preferably your wife--schedule your appointments.

Does your wife feel insecure at times because of your time commitments? Does she (or the children) need to compete with the Lord's work for your attention? If you are unsure, then they probably do--ask her about it! If the answer is yes, then authorize her to schedule your time, especially for activities that take you away from your home overnight or longer. If you often feel pressured, driven by guilt to have to fill every half hour of your time with work, you are taking on too many responsibilities; some of the things you are doing are not God's will. Give your wife authority to schedule regular sabbaths (the equivalent of one day a week spent with the family, when your mind is not on the work). During another week, make up for special events that would cause undue hardship if missed.

Start managing your time wisely right now, by recording your plans to do so in your ARFs. Pray for daily self-discipline to follow God's priorities.

109. Make practical plans now for reproductive *organization.*

With love born of the Holy Spirit, you and your disciples should be able to organize the body of Christ to enable it to reproduce normally, by doing the things listed below.

Mark the *helps for normal church reproduction* that you expect to give attention:

☐ If you are a missionary from the outside, disciple potential national leaders as you build up the growing body of Christ through them.

Do not try to do all the teaching, pastoring, and decision-making yourself; model it, then step back and let your own "Timothy" do the work. Enable many others to begin teaching and shepherding in their own homes. Provide Bible reading schedules for these *protoleaders* to use to teach in their homes and in small groups modeled after the family. Set up discipleship "chains" (you teach one of the men, and he in turn teaches others). For example, help your "Timothy" set up a regular time of Bible study in his home, then encourage him to help another newer man do the same in his home. These two links in a discipleship chain will often keep multiplying. New churches often suffer and fail from "one link" discipling chains, which involve no multiplication. All the believers are linked directly to one overworked church planter. They watch the church planter do all the discipling until he collapses from exhaustion.

☐ Disciple able, mature men (elder types).

Avoid training single, young men in pioneer fields as pastors. Train men who qualify better as "elders" (or shepherds; see Titus 1:5-9). In a pioneer field it is hard to find men who meet all the requirements, so we train the best ones that God gives us, using the Bible's guidelines as our criteria. Remember, they must be able to teach others. As a general rule, new churches in pioneer fields where there are no experienced pastoral leaders or elders yet get along better if led by several provisional elders. They are provisional in the sense that they are too new to be considered permanent elders or pastors. (Notice Acts 14:23, where Paul named fairly new believers as elders, for new churches in a pioneer field.)

☐ Organize after--not before--you know exactly what you will do.

Avoid detailed rules and bylaws until they are obviously needed; discard them as soon as they are no longer necessary.

☐ Keep evaluating your progress ruthlessly.

We need to have our goal fixed on the horizon, but also to keep developing the path as we go along. We constantly evaluate our progress as we work toward the goal, but we also allow for real breakthroughs when progress seems to be blocked. This forces us to explore new ways around the obstacles. As Scoggins puts it, "We have found, in our experience with house churches, that such 'horizon travel' leaves plenty of room for innovation, new initiatives, and a great deal of looking to the Lord!"

☐ Deploy missionaries on the basis of their *strengths* (not of *need* as other over-worked missionaries see it).

Avoid placing new workers in an area simply because there is a "need." (Where is there *not* a need??) Let them minister in a situation that maximizes their gifts and talents, not simply to keep the organization or mere programs functioning smoothly. Failure to do this is a common error of mission agency field supervisors and results in many missionaries "washing out" or "burning out" unnecessarily.

☐ Apply the biblical pattern of organization: namely, cooperation among those with different gifts.

The Western, secular, institutional pattern of specialization separates persons with different gifts or ministries, forming independent and often competitive commissions, departments, or branches. This type of organization very often stifles church reproduction. We help people with divergent gifts to find ways to cooperate, ways that open new vistas for effective ministry.

The people in a team or in a church needs a vision for what they believe God desires them to accomplish through their gifts. Once a vision is established, each person needs to find his or her place in accomplishing it. Remember "horizon travel." As people are added, the vision will need fine-tuning as each one brings his or her special gift to bear. Over time, the vision will change as we travel from one horizon to the next; God does not let us see the entire future but leads us from one phase to another.

☐ Motivate volunteer workers by enabling them, once discipled, to set their own goals and performance standards.

The underlying motive for all true Christian service is love for Jesus, who said, "If you love me, obey my commands" (John 14:15). Once this discipling mentality of loving obedience is established in the entire body, help volunteer workers to visualize and achieve what God wants them to do, out of love and self-initiative, rather than pushing them, offering rewards, threatening, using organizational clout or competition (remember that competition, in the sense of rivalry, is condemned in Scripture).

☐ As taught in 1 Peter 5:1-5 and Hebrew 13:17, have gifted shepherds with a servant's heart make crucial decisions for a church or group.

Do not rely on majority rule (except in matters requiring a congregational vote for legal reasons). Scripture and history show that the majority seldom vote for the cross-bearing, faith-stretching disciple's route; they typically choose the more secure, traditional, least demanding route. The Kingdom of God on earth (the church) is not a democracy but a monarchy. Reproductive discipling requires loving authority, in which the strong leader is a humble servant of all (Matt. 20:25-28). Many sound discipling programs have been scrapped because their participants submitted to the majority rule within their church or denomination. Let Jesus be our King!

☐ Develop body life between new churches and groups.

Church multiplication thrives on loving relationships between churches. Scripture reveals nothing of the independent spirit that some American missionaries impart to a new church. They mean well, but they are from a culture that idealizes individualism and personal rights above the rights of the society.

Scoggins relates:

We set up "fellowships" of house churches. Each fellowship is a network of from two to six cooperating house churches. The leaders meet together regularly for fellowship, training, counsel, and discussion of decisions that might affect the other house churches in the fellowship. The congregations all meet together, usually monthly. The relationships established between the leaders help in preventing a congregation from developing ingrown or "cultic" devotion to a strong leader, as well as enabling older elders to mentor younger ones. These congregational relationships reduce the number of failures of the house churches.

The New Testament consistently emphasizes developing loving, cooperative, edifying body life between churches or groups of believers. Christ's body is not a local congregation, although that is where practice of loving unity starts, among persons with different gifts and interests. For example, when the persecution started in apostolic times, the primitive churches in Jerusalem and Ephesus became clusters of closely knit, cooperating house churches. Their organization, like that of modern churches in highly restricted fields, resembled an underground crime network. In restricted fields we do not form large congregations, but an underground network of tiny house churches.

☐ Trust the Holy Spirit to motivate new leaders.

Do not fear that false doctrine will automatically

creep into rapidly reproducing groups or churches. History proves the opposite. Healthy, normally reproductive churches or cell groups are loyal to their disciplers and are oriented to obedience to Christ; false doctrine seldom is a problem. In contrast, churches that are overprotected by foreign leaders who are suspicious of false doctrine creeping in every time they turn their backs provoke a rebellious spirit that opens the window for all kinds of rare birds to fly in.

☐ Do not fear to encourage a new leader to take initiative simply because he has weaknesses-- build on his strengths.

Trusting the Holy Spirit, we build on what a potential leader can do; we release him to do it, instead of building rules around him to make him "safe." David was a great leader because God built on his strengths, not his obvious weaknesses. Especially in a pioneer field, use the best men that God gives you. There is no perfect leader.

Scoggins emphasizes:

> In our experience, strong men have strong weaknesses. If we develop good relationships between the leaders of a church, God uses other elders to offset those weaknesses, so that the strong leader does not become independent and proud but rather sees his need for his fellow elders. Whether serving on a team or in a house church fellowship, the leaders need to set the pace in relying on others to help us in our weaknesses. As we become more aware of our own weaknesses, we become more willing to mobilize other leaders with glaring weaknesses. We find more and more frequently that we need to rely on their strengths!

☐ Delegate pastoral responsibilities.

Let men with pastoral potential develop their gifts. Model pastoral skills for them. Give them the tools to study the Bible to teach its truths to others, especially the ability to do inductive Bible study. Help them to lead disciples at all levels to multiply themselves and their church or group.

☐ Help each potential pastor to clarify personal objectives.

Enable him to define his God-given goals and the little, intermediate steps he needs to keep moving toward them.

☐ Evaluate your progress by measuring results, not efforts.

Define goals in terms of concrete results expected. Help the leaders of each team, group, or church to evaluate its progress in terms of such God-given results. Measuring efforts does not tell you if you are progressing toward your goals. By efforts we mean the things we do to win people for Christ and edify the church (meetings, classes, lessons, reading, programs, crusades, etc.). By concrete results we mean converts baptized, new churches born, new classes started, daily prayer and regular, sacrificial giving begun by families, new disciples mobilized for ministry, new Bible studies *begun* (the on-going classes themselves are efforts), and transformation of lives and families. In short, loving obedience leads to *efforts* made in the power of the Holy Spirit, which lead to *results*. This chain of cause and effect cannot be short-circuited.

☐ If in a pioneer field, use a simple form of worship service that new leaders with limited training can imitate and pass on at once to others they train.

Use a worship style that new elders can lead themselves with a minimum of supervision, one that is culturally relevant. For example, if they are new believers, they should not do pulpit oratory; it will make them proud. They should celebrate the Lord's Supper weekly, read Scripture, exhort, and tell Bible stories that their disciplers have helped them prepare.

☐ Develop a *midwife mentality* for reproducing churches.

Especially if your church planting team is working cross-culturally, you are there to help those in the other culture reproduce on their own initiative in the power of the Holy Spirit. We do not cause the reproduction ourselves. The new congregation should take all responsibility as soon as possible for giving birth to still other churches and training their pastors. The stronger the team itself is organizationally, the harder it is sometimes to keep its hands off the new church and let the infant church take initiative in the power of the Holy Spirit.

☐ Accept accountability only to a leader who encourages you in a ministry that makes use of your gifts and strengths, in fulfillment of what God is calling you to do.

Again, prayerfully verify a potential field supervisor's attitude before committing your life's career to an organization, church, or team.

☐ Become experts in discipling on all levels: with pre-Christians, new Christians, older Christians, and leaders.

Most of the world's remaining unreached fields need church planters and evangelists skilled in personal discipling. In Muslim, Communist, and other restricted and unchurched fields where Christian gatherings are prohibited--which represent one-third of the world's people--missionaries must work without classrooms or pulpits. A church that practices biblical discipling does not need a special evangelism program or department. Evangelism is integrated into every aspect of the church's life, just as Paul includes it in the normal work of a pastor (2 Tim. 4:1-5).

110. **Implementation:** Note your plans for reproductive organization and servant leadership. Mark applicable items in Appendix D *Items to Review.* Also, note your *general* plans below:

_____

_____

_____

_____

_____

_____

_____

_____

_____

_____

_____

_____

_____

Chapter 13. The Viewpoint of the Small Group

<u>**Recommended Bible Study:**</u> Exodus 18:13-27. Look for reasons for small groups.

Patterson relates how he got suspicious pastors to name small group leaders:

Forming small groups in Honduran churches goes against their culture, which favors one central authority. Our pastors instinctively feared that group leaders would usurp their authority. So the churches grew no

Don't develop new leaders in your church!

They change the peck order and you lose out!

larger than what a one-man nucleus could group around himself; most churches, led by one part-time lay pastor, reached a plateau at around fifty members. Having met to change this, we built a fire on the dirt floor of the chapel, which represented hell. Then we placed paper "sheep" on four chairs a few feet apart and asked the pastor to guard them against several "wolves" that we named, who sought to steal the sheep from the chairs one at a time and throw them into

the fire. While the shepherd guarded one chair, a wolf would rob a sheep from another; soon nearly all of the sheep were cast into hell. John Calvin would have winced at the theology, but we did make our point. We asked the pastor to name an elder for each chair, to help him shepherd the sheep. When we turned the wolves loose again, not one sheep was lost; instead, all the wolves were put to death. We read Jethro's advice to Moses in Exodus 18 to name group leaders, and then we prayed for God's leading. Soon small groups appeared in many churches, which started growing again.

111. Plan activities now to enable reproductive discipleship in small groups or *cells*.

If you plan to form or lead small groups for reproductive discipleship, prepare an *Activity Review File* for a small group. Such a file for a small ministry group might include the following activities:

Mark applicable *activities for reproductive discipling in cell groups*:

☐ <u>Practice evangelism in the homes of friends and relatives.</u>

Remember, the best evangelists are new believers. Mobilize them to witness to their unsaved friends and relatives. Keep the network of communication spreading. The most effective evangelists for children are normally their father or mother. Mobilize them to evangelize their children. It is normally easier to mobilize new believers and parents to evangelize their own people through small, family-oriented groups.

☐ Confirm each new believer's salvation without delay.

Scoggins reports:

We teach new believers from Acts 2:37-41 three steps to confirm their salvation: repentance, baptism, and being added to the body of believers. We teach older believers their responsibility to shepherd new believers into the body. Since converts are being shepherded individually in love, we encourage them to do the same with those that come to faith through their witness. In some cases an older believer who leads another to faith through these early steps will actually baptize his "disciple." When a husband comes to faith quite some time before his wife, he may be encouraged to baptize her. When appropriate, we authorize fathers who lead their children to faith to baptize them.

Disciples are taught by their mentors to become a part of the body. Since we emphasize the relational aspect of being part of the body of believers, we use a covenant to spell out the responsibility that believers have for each other as they become church members. When new believers understand that they are joining God's covenant people, their respective mentors recommend them for membership. The mentors affirm before the church the faith of the new believers and their readiness to contribute to the life of the body. Upon the recommendation of a mentor, a new believer affirms his or her desire to abide by the covenant, and the body affirms its desire to receive and nurture this new brother or sister. We pattern this covenant ceremony after the vows in a wedding and follow it with a feast to celebrate.

By having those who lead people to faith also disciple them into the body, discipleship chains are established early and naturally in the lives of new believers. They naturally go to their mentor when they need help. Likewise, mentors feel more responsible for new believers when "their" believer gets into trouble.

Patterson also relates how the Honduran churches confirmed new convert's salvation:

We discovered that new believers felt accepted by God when they were accepted by his church. They heeded his Word more eagerly after baptism. Normally one was baptized by the main pastor of the church, or an authorized elder. This was followed by a joyful reception. We tried to give the same importance to baptism as the apostles did (Acts 2:37-42).

☐ Mobilize fathers to pastor their own families.

This includes praying with their wives and children, reading the Word together, and telling their children Bible stories. Scoggins's churches do this by offering daily reading schedules to be used in the home, as mentioned above. The questions are practical and show how the Word of God applies to individual, family, and group needs.

☐ Help fathers of families and group teachers to apply the Word of God continually to individual, family, and group needs.

We ask them to do inductive study of the Word, instead of simply telling them what a passage says. We ask them to study it themselves and return to the next discipling session with what they found. For example, we don't simply assign Exodus 18, for example, to our group leaders, but we ask them to examine it to find out why group leaders were necessary for Moses, and for churches today. (Note that the Bible studies recommended in this guide ask you to look for something.)

☐ Help each member of the group to obey all the commands of Jesus, including celebrating the Lord's Supper regularly.

Communion may be served in small groups or together with the entire church; group leaders make sure all their members are taking part in the Lord's Supper regularly. It should be celebrated with the solemnity it deserves, following a time of self-examination and confession of sins, allowing its own God-given drama and mystery to have their effect.

☐ Each group leader trains apprentices as assistant leaders.

These assistants not only help lead the groups but also start new groups. The church grows by addition and multiplication. Remember, growth by addition simply adds converts to the existing body; growth by multiplication creates a new nucleus around which new members are more easily grouped. A new daughter church or a newly formed home group normally attracts new or pre-Christians more readily than does a large group made up mainly of mature Christians. And, normally, the easiest way for a new group leader to get started is to serve as an apprentice to a more experienced leader.

☐ Arrange for the assistant or new leaders who are inexperienced teachers to lead small group discussions.

Inexperienced leaders can start teaching in an effective way simply by having them ask key questions about a Bible passage that their group will read.

Some *questions to make Bible reading applicable to our lives:*

✔ What does it urge us to do or to avoid?

✔ Is there a direct command from God?

✔ What promise does it have for us?

✔ How can it help us to be more like Jesus?

✔ What is your plan to put it into action? (With whom? When?)

☐ Form a new group each time an old one grows large.

A group is too big when it can no longer give attention to each member's personal needs during the meetings (normally after it grows beyond about fourteen adults).

☐ Group leaders meet regularly (preferably weekly) with their main pastor.

He helps them plan their next meetings and holds them accountable for group activities and seeing that all members of his group are personally discipled by someone.

☐ Cultivate loving fellowship within the group.

Give special attention to both pre-Christians and new Christians.

☐ Deal with common personal needs and apply the Word of God to specific individual or family problems.

Arrange for counseling within the groups for personal or family problems, such as grief after a death, drug or alcohol addiction, broken family relationships, divorce, or injured emotions.

☐ Help all members to discover and practice their different spiritual gifts (evangelism, prophecy, mercy, giving, faith, healing, etc.).

Scoggins relates:

We emphasize to small house churches that all the spiritual gifts needed for effective nurture of the body may not be available in a single church. As a result our house churches network together so that gifts can flow between the churches. This is especially important in the ministry of counseling, or what we call "soul healing." But we find it true in other areas as well.

☐ Pray for each other.

Pray especially for the sick and those oppressed by demons. Give personal attention to, and pray for, any person present who might feel left out. This may require forming still smaller prayer groups during the meetings.

☐ Give offerings for special projects.

In small groups that are not themselves a house church, accounting of these funds should be done through the church.

112. Make plans now to enable the *birth* of small groups, or of churches which start as small groups or cells.

Give lots of loving help to a group during its birth, or to a church that starts as a group.

Neglect of the items reviewed below commonly causes the abortion of brand new groups and churches in embryo. Mark those you plan to give special attention:

☐ Visualize a clear model for the kind of group or church you want, and what God wants it to do.

Remember, God must enable you to see the new congregation doing these activities, in your heart.

Otherwise, there is no way you can *lead* the people, because you do not see where God wants them to go. You can only *teach* them.

If you are starting a church, begin at once with the group to act like a church--obey all of Jesus' commands (do not have a mere "preaching point"). Remember also to have a definite, formal beginning and end to each worship service. Celebrate the Lord's Supper regularly with solemnity and give tithes and offerings. Scoggins adds:

> Each of our house churches develops a vision statement that attempts to see about six months into the future. It is written with specific goals for reproduction (starting new evangelistic gathering groups and reproducing disciples, leaders, and new congregations) as well as activities that enable the church to progress toward these goals. Several times in the course of the six-month period the group will have a "health check" to evaluate its progress and/or the vision. In this way new members also are brought up to date on the vision.

☐ Keep evangelizing during the birth phase (don't stop just because you have begun holding worship services).

Gather people from the same culture and social level. Do not depend on your newly begun worship services alone to attract people to Christ.

☐ Share pastoral responsibilities and hold volunteer workers accountable to do their jobs.

Keep training potential leaders on the job as assistants. Apply Titus 1:5-9 to recognize those assistants who are ready to lead their own groups. If you detect competition between the elders, workers, or trainees, deal with it firmly at once, in the Spirit of Philippians 2:1-18. Help each minister and his wife to agree together on her role in the church or group.

☐ Avoid discouraging new workers with too many chores.

In small groups, limit refreshments to something simple; do not make it hard to host the meetings. Avoid serving meals. Take turns caring for the children if they distract. Hold the meetings in the home of someone besides the main leader so that no one thinks he owns the group. Scoggins explains:

> By keeping meetings to a minimum, we avoid overstaying our welcome in a particular home. We try to have only one community meeting weekly in a central home. We hold other meetings for gathering (evangelism) and ministry in other homes as the Lord directs.

☐ Be creative in how you apply the Word to the needs and level of spiritual maturity of the members of the group.

Be sensitive to the fears and doubts of new members. Do not simply study the Bible; apply it to specific needs and ministry opportunities. Avoid long, formal sermons. Encourage group participation in the studies, including the children and young people. Use other ways of teaching God's Word besides formal pulpit oratory (interpretive reading, discussion, story telling, poetry, drama, composing and singing songs, brief informal meditations, exhortation, spontaneous discussion or comments). Do not have new leaders preach formally (it often causes pride).

Scoggins relates:

> In most of our house churches, we find that lectures are counterproductive to learning. Instead, people learn by interacting with the Word in a discussion. This works especially well when they have had a reading schedule to follow in their homes during the week. Sometimes a lecture is called for, such as for a meeting to train more mature believers rather than a Sunday community meeting.

☐ If you are meeting in homes, avoid meeting too often or too long in one home (wearing out your welcome) or moving too frequently from one house to another (losing track of where to meet).

☐ Avoid outside speakers--regardless of how "good" they may be--who come with objectives other than what your group has.

☐ Prohibit business dealings (selling insurance, etc.) during meetings.

☐ Impart a vision for reproducing home groups, especially to all new believers.

☐ Imitate the example of the Apostolic church.

Ministry in homes, including the celebration of the Lord's Supper, is illustrated in Acts 2:46, 5:42, 20:20, and Romans 16:5.

113. **Implementation:** Mark the items you will review later, in Appendix E. Add detailed plans now to your ARFs to mobilize small group leaders to reproduce themselves in new leaders of new groups or house churches. Note your general plans below:

_____

_____

_____

_____

_____

_____

_____

_____

_____

_____

_____

_____

_____

_____

14. The Viewpoint of the House Church

We use the term "house church" in this chapter, even though the church may meet in an office or other limited space. The crucial point is that because of its commitment to growth by multiplication, it chooses not to seek facilities for an ever-increasing attendance.

Recommended Bible Study: Acts 2:46, 5:42, 20:20, and Romans 16:5. Look for cases of, and circumstances surrounding, the practice of worshiping in homes.

114. Verify circumstances objectively that normally show when house churches are needed.

The question arises, *When should we plant a house church with the intention that it remain indefinitely as a house church and not seek a building?* This raises other questions. What specific and obvious circumstances warrant the multiplication of small churches as a priority objective? Where does the typical Western assumption come from, that the lack of a lot of people *in one building* means failure? (It does not come from Scripture; the early church in Jerusalem, like that of Ephesus and other major cities, consisted of clusters of tiny house churches.) So where do the assumptions come from, that we must have a building, or a large crowd in one place, or that we

A *house* church???

That's for the buzzards!

I won't worship without stained glass !

must pay one professional pastor full time, or that he must be trained in an institution outside the body of Christ the church? All of these assumptions are *culturally based traditions*. The assumption that the Spirit of God is limited without these things is contrary to faith; it causes enormous damage to the church and frequently stifles growth and reproduction in Christ's body.

Our decision to form, remain as, or discontinue a house church should not come from feelings *pro* or *con* about church buildings. No inherent virtue or evil attaches either to church buildings or to house churches as such. Scripture mentions that the early Christians met both in the temple and in houses; God gives us liberty to do both. Our motive should rather be to obey Jesus and allow God to keep the work growing and reproducing, without restricting it humanly. Under some circumstances house churches offer more liberty in the Spirit to mobilize new leaders and put into practice spiritual gifts that allow church growth, edification, and reproduction. In other circumstances church buildings offer more liberty. In some societies churches reproduce more rapidly when they have buildings. For example, in some third world countries small chapels are often built by the people themselves at very little cost, out of materials available locally, causing no limitations on ministry. In some third world fields, when a church outgrows its chapel, it is more common to build another nearby, and culturally more acceptable. This is usually done with less trouble where churches have a *plurality of elders* and where sister churches remain in close contact with each other so as not to break relationships between brothers in Christ when a new church forms. Scoggins notes:

> The plurality of elders enables older leaders constantly to train younger ones. When new churches begin, these older elders, perhaps in a different church, still serve as a mentor or discipler to the younger men. This networking of leadership between churches serves to give stability to the leadership and the congregations in which they serve. It will also tend to work against the independent spirit that often serves to foster competition between evangelical churches. We have found that where the leadership is networking closely together in a cooperative spirit, there is less sheep stealing. Where people may move from one church to another, it can be done with much encouragement as we see God's hand using the resources of one church to bless another.

Our goal is to be certain that all barriers to what the Holy Spirit might desire to do are removed. If he desires to bring explosive growth and reproduction, we desire to have ministry methods in place that are flexible enough to grow with him and not restrict his blessing. Such methods need plans for multiplication and not simply addition. We want to give liberty for the Spirit of God to mobilize workers to evangelize and edify, without restrictions imposed by buildings or the lack of them. In some cases, a rapidly growing house church may see a building as a detriment to growth; later they might decide that a building would be helpful. Unfortunately, many Western churches seldom consider the alternative to building, as their cultural inertia moves them toward centralizing rather than decentralizing.

115. Be content with being a house church if that is how God is leading.

Be content with the goal of multiplying a cluster of small house churches, and do not to try to act, in the meantime, like a large church or gear plans to becoming one large church. After the church reproduces a cluster of house churches, they can rent a building if God so leads and then meet as often as they like in united celebration, easily paying a pastor to help coordinate the entire network of churches and help train house church leaders. In the meantime, be content to be a good house church; act like a small congregation and enjoy the close fellowship of a little community.

House churches are often devastated by a leader who aspires to pastor a large church that pays a full salary and meets in a building. He inevitably leads a house church into an impasse: they cannot grow large enough in a house to afford a building, but they become too large for the house. This painful situation is made worse if the leader discourages multiplying to start new house churches, fearing that the group might become even smaller and move even further away from his goal of a building and full-time salary. Such a pastor nearly always pushes a house church into a building prematurely or fails to use a style of teaching, worship, or organization that is conducive to small house churches. He uses a style of leadership that other potential leaders in the house church cannot imitate, making it impossible to multiply other house churches.

116. To keep multiplying, prepare new house church leaders as on-the-job apprentices.

We can prepare new leaders more easily if we enable all heads of families to pastor their own spouses and children. Provide regular Bible reading for them, a list of key Bible events or persons, with a reading for each day of the year. After reading and discussing a Bible passage with his family, a family head can often easily lead discussion during a house church worship service. Many who are inexperienced in teaching quickly gain the needed practice to lead small groups this way. Family heads might teach the house church body this way in rotation. This works when we place strong emphasis on shepherding our families in our homes. This family approach produces new and potential leaders, who are overlooked in more traditional churches and who make it possible to multiply sister churches quickly.

117. Take advantage of the small group atmosphere to enable entire families to participate in worship.

Help the people to sing and discuss the Word of God more freely by sitting in a circle and using discussion-type teaching rather than pulpit oratory. Include the children; they might sing, recite poems or Psalms, read or recite Bible verses from memory, or act out biblical stories.

118. Discern positive, objective indications of the need to multiply house churches rather than erect, expand or rent a building.

How do we detect the circumstances that favor house church multiplication? Objective, obvious criteria are very often overlooked when we decide to build or to meet indefinitely in homes. These criteria vary from culture to culture. Some common guidelines to recognize when you should opt for house church multiplication are listed below. They should help you decide whether to build, expand or rent facilities for one congregation, or to multiply house churches.

Mark *indications of the need for house churches* that apply to your church:

☐ Lack of funds for buildings.

As obvious as this is, the house church option is often overlooked, even though money is lacking to rent or build the kind of buildings needed to house the church(es) under consideration. As a result, new churches often fail, especially in urban areas, because of the financial burden. Scoggins recalls:

> One of the driving forces in our decision to start house churches was our limited resources for renting or building in an urban area. Most people living in urban areas have limited resources, and land values are high. As a result we settled on a house church strategy to keep financial pressure from dictating the policy of the church. Too often money becomes the deciding factor in what does or does not get done. In our house churches the financial question became irrelevant.

☐ Persecution by hostile authorities.

Where churches must gather underground, the need for house churches is obvious. In Muslim fields, in China and southern Asia, millions of believers meet in tiny house churches.

☐ Lack of funds for *full-time* pastoral leaders.

Salaried, professional ministry is more often associated with church buildings and the larger congregations that attend them. Centralized organization--usually more costly--is more often associated with a building, while decentralized organization more typically lends itself to a network of house churches. When money cannot be made available for such staff without compromising other essential ministries, let us prayerfully consider the house church option. Scoggins explains:

> None of the elders in our house churches are supported. All are bi-vocational and supply the needs of their families through normal jobs (from doctors to truck drivers). Since each elder oversees only three or four families, all of whom are available for service, this is not an excessive burden.

☐ Inability to get the "critical mass" needed to launch a growing church in a building, with people used to a large attendance.

Most churches that opt for centralized organization and a building need, in the middle-class American culture, from between thirty and sixty committed adult believers before they can begin public worship. A smaller number gets them off on the wrong foot; they lack the personnel to maintain the image and programs needed to attract more people to that kind of church. House churches, in contrast, can start with a small number of committed believers. In Scoggins's experience, a house church often starts with only two or three families.

☐ The *vision* to form a cluster of house churches.

An isolated, lonely small house church seldom survives long. Scoggins affirms:

> Independent house churches are fraught with dangers. They easily develop cultic tendencies that go unchecked, since their is no accountability beyond themselves. They usually fail to reproduce and become ingrown. They also

often become self-centered and elitist; God's spirit is no longer able to use them. They collapse, leaving in their wake a string of broken, embittered believers. For these reasons, we focus on starting networks of cooperating house churches rather than individual house churches. Interaction between house churches brings stability and perspective. In times of blessing, we can share resources with others who are struggling. In times of trial, others are there to help us.

The ability to multiply depends much on the leader's ability to train new elders/copastors to keep up with the growth and multiplication. A church planting team lacking this ability will in time be unable to provide the leadership for a house church movement. An effective team thinks in terms of reproducing house churches. Just one house church is like one baseball player facing the other team's nine alone. A house church needs the warmth and identity of a cluster of sister house churches in close fellowship with it. They meet together for a united celebration (perhaps once a month), and their leaders meet even more frequently to coordinate the work.

☐ Ability to form an inter-church network to keep relationships intact when churches grow too large for a house and must multiply.

Women generally feel it more keenly when continued growth by multiplication forces them to break existing relationships. These relationships are maintained through inter-church organization. People must be available in a potential mother church, then, who are experienced or can be trained to disciple newer Christians and leaders in the new daughter church (including women and teenagers).

☐ Ability to take care of children and to provide opportunities for teenagers to meet other young people.

For teenagers, this usually requires some kind of inter-church network.

☐ Leadership that can resist strong opposition to the house church mentality.

Where traditions are very strong in favor of buildings, people sometimes stubbornly assume that a building is necessary, regardless of obvious, compelling reasons to the contrary. In this case, leaders cannot allow the two philosophies to mix. If they open the door even a crack to consider a larger building, such people will insist on it without thinking it through. Deeply embedded traditions sometimes keep people from feeling that they have worshiped seriously unless they have done so in a church building. In spite of conscientious biblical instruction on the true meaning of worship, they simply cannot adapt to a house church. Church planters should be sensitive to this mentality; if the people they are committed to working with simply will not follow them into a house church ministry, they may have to allow for a building, even though circumstances indicate that it may hinder the work later on. In more traditional societies, a cluster of house churches needs at least one strong, popular leader who successfully resists this tide.

119. Discern *danger signs* warning that one ever-growing church centered in a building is stifling freedom in the Spirit.

Mark any applicable *signs of warning that your church may be growing too large in one facility*:

✔ *Increased frustration expressed by persons who feel their ministries are being restricted.*

Such complaints from otherwise non-critical persons may indicate that a building (or the centralized organization associated with it) is restricting freedom in the Spirit to serve and exercise spiritual gifts. These complaints may be God's voice for us, urging us to consider starting more daughter churches in houses. If the churches of an entire community or culture

✔ *Conscientious objections to investing tithes and offerings in material buildings.*

Sometimes, even though funds for buildings are available, a congregation places higher priority on giving to ministries or workers. This conviction is often due to a healthy reaction against excessive institutionalism. The house church option often enables such Christians to achieve large church

But some of these problems arise in house churches, too.

But we deal with them easier in small churches.

And a leader who errs doesn't drag down as many with him.

growth and maintain their non-institutional priorities at the same time. Scoggins says:

> Generally in the house church, money is allocated to people. Most of our house churches use only about 20 percent of the giving for administrative purposes. The rest goes to benevolent needs and to missions.

✔ *New workers walk on eggs in order to develop or expand a ministry.*

An organization is too big or too centralized when newer members--or older members desiring to do something new--have to play church politics to avoid hurting feelings, breaking rules, or offending persons in power. This condition is also common in house churches whose leaders are legalistic or power hungry. Sadly, there may even be a lack of interest and fervor in following up newcomers.

Often, in large churches with attendance of a thousand or more, the amount of evangelism done *outside the church in the community* drops practically to zero. This also happens in some older, ingrown house churches.

✔ *"Maintenance" replaces outreach.*

We smell danger when we give more thought and energy to keeping existing programs running smoothly than to reaching out to the unchurched community. Programs exist without "sunset clauses" (about when to terminate them) or any commitment to evaluate their continued effectiveness. A church's activities simply take on a life of their own, whether or not they accomplish the purposes for which they were initiated. When someone suggests to scrap a program, more noise is made about who might be offended and who we might lose than how we can better win the lost! An obvious indicator of this isolation and maintenance syndrome is exhaustion of leaders. Ministry becomes a chore rather than a joy.

✔ *Planning sessions revolve more around keeping the organization running smoothly than around spiritual and pastoral concerns.*

Leaders spend more time discussing how they can improve or protect the image of the church, save or raise funds, maintain programs or avoid problems, than making plans of an immediate, pastoral nature for edifying specific people and dealing with new opportunities.

✔ *Rules proliferate.*

Much time is spent revising constitutions, by-laws, or other policies in order to maintain control, safeguard from possible dangers, and avoid problems; leaders rush to surround innovators with rules to protect the existing conformity; members not in places of leadership complain that the church is run by human policies instead of being led by the Holy Spirit; and members fear to suggest changes lest they be considered divisive.

✔ Organizing for an innovation takes longer and longer.

Everything goes slower to open doors for new ministries; channels for decision become bureaucratic, and leaders are more concerned with how things operate than for whom or why. Decisions made from the top down discourage individual initiative. Often leaders make great decisions that never get implemented because of apathy on the part of the congregation. The clarion cry becomes

"We don't want to make a mistake"--as if no decision or delayed decisions are not mistakes. Another cry is "We don't want to move too fast"--as if it is never wrong to move too slowly. The book of Acts shows that the Spirit of God often moves fast. What would be the traditional church's response if 3,000 were added in one day? They would creak and grown and complain until many leave out the back door, then sigh with relief as things get back to "normal"--nothing new happening.

✔ Potential leaders are competing.

One must "fight to the top" for a position in which his spiritual gifts can be used freely--a complaint also heard in house churches when their leaders overcontrol.

✔ *The percentage of members in places of leadership declines.*

A chronic shortage of leaders in touch with the local community stifles outreach. A church fails to train and reproduce enough of its own really effective leaders for essential ministries, especially ministries that mobilize new believers for evangelism of their friends and relatives.

✔ *People rely more and more on paid staff.*

The complaint becomes frequent that volunteer workers or leaders can no longer be counted on for key positions.

✔ *Programs receive more attention than people do.*

✔ *Funds for buildings and paid staff are getting unbalanced attention.*

Signs appear that people feel bullied into giving more and more; other areas of pastoral concern get insufficient attention in business or board meetings.

✔ *Unsaved visitors return less.*

Non-Christians and visitors seeking a new church sometimes fail to find friends who readily receive them into the group, or they may feel that their spiritual gifts are not wanted--also a problem in house churches when they become ingrown.

✔ *Church multiplication (i.e., the forming of daughter and granddaughter churches) is nonexistent or declining.*

✔ *Formation of effective small groups becomes harder.*

A large and growing church needs more and more small groups that give real pastoral care on a personal and family level. These small groups draw in new converts and mobilize new leaders for growing needs. When a church fails to mobilize such small groups in spite of heroic efforts by its leaders, it has probably long since passed the time when they should have begun multiplying house churches.

If many of the above criteria apply to you, prayerfully consider, and plan for, clusters of house churches. Remember our liberty to have or not to have a church building. Avoid any assumption that we must have a building in order for God's Spirit to work.

120. In new or embryonic churches gear most of the Bible teaching to building relationships between members and leaders.

The carnal attitudes, ambitions, power struggles, selfishness and indifference underlying the problems in larger churches (listed above) also arise in house churches. In fact, they arise *more readily*. The intimate family atmosphere makes it impossible to hide them! The greater opportunities to lead and serve also bring them out at quickly. Welcome this. Let the intimacy and flexibility of the small congregation facilitate correction as the problems arise. *Most of the Bible teaching* during a church's embryo and infant stages and certainly as long as new leaders are developing (often for more than a year), deals frankly with these attitudes in a family atmosphere of loving acceptance. Scoggins' new groups spend weeks applying the New Testament "one another" verses to their group life, especially to relationships between members in preparation for *covenanting* together as a house church.

121. Once a new group decides to become a house church, affirm the commitment to form a small, loving, family-like house church with a serious, positive *covenant.*

House churches must covenant together to love, forgive, nurture and minister to one another as a family. According to Scoggins, when a new group prepares and signs this covenant, the church is considered to be born. The covenant--call it what you may--rather than a traditional constitution with its legal overtones, defines in detail how members live and serve the Lord as a caring body. Every detail of it is taught slowly from Scripture, discussed openly and prayerfully by the emerging group, and agreed upon by every member of the group. Make sure a new church in embryo understands God's covenants in the Old and New Testaments, so they can covenant together to define the kind of church they will form, and how they will behave toward each other as members.

This covenant is not to define doctrine nor prohibit sins. It is positive, emphasizing their love, forgiveness and ministry for each other. As mentioned above, the churches should study and discuss the ''one another'' passages in the New Testament for several weeks while they are learning to work together and recognizing their own new leaders. During this time, as they make decisions and explore their gift-based ministries, the carnality of the members and the weaknesses of the leaders always become apparent. This helps them to discuss and write their own covenant in a context of reality, struggle and progress, which makes it practical for future guidance. The house church, thus born through a process of joyful and tearful struggle, continues as a *closely knit family type community.*

122. Form small ''gathering meetings'' for unbelievers, led by the converts themselves.

One independent small house church alone will not survive for long. Nor is it normal for it *not* to reproduce. How do we make sure a house church reproduces? Simply mobilize each convert to witness for Jesus to his family and friends, and follow them up in a small group context in their own neighborhood--that is, keep multiplying ''gathering groups.''

A gathering group normally has one, two or three families (or up to 5 or 6 singles) and is strictly for unbelievers. It is not for worship nor in-depth Bible study. Older Christians who know their Bible well and have already overcome the problems common to new Christians make the others feel ill at ease.

Sometimes these gathering meetings are born when a still-unconverted head of a household begins reading Bible stories to his own family or in some other way

teaches the Word, and prays with them, under the guidance of a discipler or evangelist.

Also, gathering meeting may be led at first by an ''outside'' church planter. But he turns leadership over to responsible converts as soon as possible, usually a head of household whom he coaches from behind the scenes. When the unbelievers in gathering groups convert, some of the groups will merge and/or evolve into house churches; others will feed into existing house churches.

Do not extract converts from their social circle to take them to one large, ever-growing congregation completely outside and unrelated to their own community. Keep teaching them the importance of being nurtured by their disciplers in the small group family, and of covenanting together and serving one another within the new community which the Holy Spirit has supernaturally brought together.

As new heads of households are converted, help them start more small gathering meetings for their unsaved friends. Never stop holding these evangelistic gathering meetings. As you model *leading* these groups, do everything in a way a new man can imitate at once. By the time a convert's social network has been ''mined out'' (all his friends and relatives have been evangelized and have either received or rejected Jesus) you should have started new gathering meetings with other converts.

123. Form a *cluster* of house churches, with two or more ''servant-leaders'' in each church, who also meet regularly as an inter-church board to coordinate cooperation between churches.

When one house church has grown large enough (normally five families or 14 adults) let the converts from the gathering meetings covenant together to form another house church. Don't ''divide'' the original church unless everyone the group has discussed it fully, prayed about it and everyone involved is in agreement, including the wives of any workers (think *multiplication*; not *division*). A family may choose to go with the new group this way, to serve as its leader. Or they may decide simply to channel converts and no older members into a new nucleus for another house church. In this case an ''outside'' church planter(s) would furnish the initial leadership.

During this birth stage and often for more than a year, the new group is nurtured in love by the parent church. The mother church keeps smothering the daughter church with loving care as long as it needs it. The more experienced leaders (elders, elders-in-training or whatever you call the recognized, more mature leaders) keep discipling the new leaders and workers of the daughter churches. The more experienced women in the mother church also disciple the newer women in the daughter churches. Let the leaders (elders) of the different churches form an "overseer board" (call it also whatever you want) which meets at least once a month plus whenever there is an urgent need. They coordinate this cooperation between the churches. They also arrange for all the churches in their network to meet together regularly at convenient intervals for united worship and celebration.

For this rapid house church reproduction, each church needs more than one leader (elder, co-pastor or whatever term you choose). Usually a more experienced church planter will lead the group at first. But the quicker he turns over leadership to new, local leaders, the better. The long he waits to do this, the harder it is. He, and every elder he trains, is always training a "Timothy" or two as apprentices. And each "Timothy" must begin at once to train his own Timothies in the same church or in the daughter churches.

Often, two or more church planters work with a new church during the initial gathering or evangelism stage, then all but one move on to start new churches in a completely new area. The church planter who stays with the group trains its first new leader, who trains other leaders, (potential or "provisions" elders) then he, too, moves on. After planting the first church in an area, the church planters must go far enough away to start their next work,, so that the first church in an area will take full responsibility for starting the other churches in that area.

124. **Implementation:** Mark items in Appendix E to follow up. Record any specific plans in your ARFs, for house churches. Write any general plans or commitment now:

_____

_____

_____

_____

_____

_____

_____

_____

_____

_____

_____

Chapter 15, The Viewpoint of the Mother Church, or Sending Body

Recommended Bible Study: Acts 13:1-3. Look for what God and the church did to send a church-based missionary team.

125. Mobilize those in your church to whom God gives the apostolic gift, as *teams*.

We can expect God to give a church (or cluster of small house churches) people with the gift of apostleship--the cross-cultural missionary gift to plant new churches in another area. We mobilize these people to use their gift to reproduce churches the same way we would mobilize people with other gifts in the body, by putting them to work using their gift. Release them to start daughter churches now.

What does a "sending church" have to do to send a team that reproduces the church at home or abroad? Let us filter out a bit of smog first by stating what a church does not need in order to multiply itself. It does not need a "missions pastor" or even a "missions committee" (they might help, however). It does not need money (it might help, however, in budget-oriented societies). It does not need to have a large membership (small churches may need to partner with sister churches, however). It does not need a high-powered executive to recruit and push people to work. Churches reproduce in virtually

Wait. We can't do the Antioch thing until we've built a strong home nest. That'll take years!

every culture and have multiplied happily without these things.

A reproductive church does need the faith and vision that it is part of the living body of Christ and that God gives it what it needs to reproduce. God gives to all living things that he has created the power to reproduce. He gives to his churches members with the necessary spiritual gifts, especially the apostolic gift to spearhead the church planting team.

If we nurture these gifts within the body with love, the Spirit of God lets us know when he wants us to separate the team, just as he did in Antioch (Acts 13). A church reproduces normally when it behaves as an obedient, healthy body that harmonizes the use of the different spiritual gifts given to it.

Patterson explains how he urged Honduran churches to reproduce:

At first our Honduran pastors insisted that it was the missionary's job to start new churches. But at the rate we were going, it would have taken three thousand years to plant churches in all the villages in our area of responsibility, if it was left to the missionaries. So we had another meeting. I explained that the mission agency was not what reproduced churches. Churches reproduce churches. I was not going to plant any more churches, but I would help them do it. They drew a large map of the villages in the area on an old piece of cardboard. Each worker signed his name by the villages for which his church would be responsible. Each worker committed himself to mobilizing a church planting team from his church. This was a turning point in our work, which God used to start the multiplication.

Help your home church to develop this team mentality among its church planters. Church-based teams sent by a loving, caring church (or cluster of sister churches) are generally more effective in reproducing churches. They work together, balancing their gifts and building relationships before going overseas, thus avoiding the number one cause of failure on the field--inability to get along with coworkers. They also maintain stronger accountability to the sending church(es) to reproduce new churches in an unreached area. More and more churches are thinking in terms of sending teams to reproduce their church. They do not leave church planting totally to the mission agencies. God is reawakening this vision in a growing number of American churches that take Acts 13:1-3 seriously. Some of them have formed the Antioch Network (may their tribe increase), *301 W. Indian School Rd. Suite A-119, Phoenix, AZ 85013.* Mission agencies can much more easily mobilize church multipliers if they are sent as teams by a church or by churches partnering together.

126. Let your church's overseas reproduction continue freely without tying it to any limiting factors.

If a church cannot afford to support those members who are gifted as apostles, it should not stop sending, nor should it assume that it needs subsidy from other churches. The bi-vocational (self-supporting) route is open to those who are gifted as apostles and is the only way to work among most of the remaining unreached peoples.

127. Provide unbiased career counseling.

Help your home church to arrange for career counseling that is unbiased. Otherwise some missionaries, counseled by recruiters and promoters of different agencies and training institutions, will be channeled unawares into existing programs, clustering missionaries in fields already reached. Let us not perpetuate the present imbalance: nearly all new missionaries go to fields already reached, and few of those who do go to new fields enter restricted areas, where the need and response is usually greater. Simply inform your potential missionaries honestly of all the options.

128. Help team members to love and appreciate the church and to know exactly what they are reproducing.

Church planters must love the church and its ministries in order to plant a reproductive daughter church. Often church planting team members have had a negative experience in a stagnant local church, or have never even been a member of a warm, active, and obedient local church. They will lack a clear concept of what they are trying to plant. Such workers are often found on church planting teams from para-church organizations (mission agencies or other groups that are not themselves churches but want to help start churches). Therefore, effective training for church planters exposes them to a good model church (especially those who lack experience in a warm, obedient church). They cannot learn essential church planting skills in a classroom.

Such schools sometimes call in experts to lecture on different aspects of church planting. If the students have little experience in a reproductive church, these lectures will make little or no measurable contribution to later church planting. Teachers who minister mainly outside the church (i.e., not integrated with a church planting team or with an existing church) sometimes do more harm than good lecturing to new church planters. Practicing one's spiritual gift (in this case, the gift of teaching) without harmonizing it with the use of other gifts given to a local body is precisely what keeps the body from reproducing. Outside speakers who present evangelism, development, or other specialized ministries without integrating them with the church may also actually make it harder for their students to plant churches.

129. Pray for God's help to persuade your coworkers to rely on your church's God-given power to grow by multiplication as well as by addition.

Recommended Bible Story: Acts 13-14. Look for what the mother church in Antioch did and how the apostles remained accountable to it (13:1-3; 14:26-28).

Church planting is an important aspect of church growth through outreach and conversion for several reasons. First, most unreached populations are best evangelized by planting many small, new churches.

Second, small, new churches do more personal evangelism per member. After a congregation reaches an ideal number for its own culture (enough members to support and carry on the work), further growth causes a decrease in evangelism in proportion to its membership. In some cultures the ideal number may be less than a hundred; in others, seven hundred to a thousand. In tightly restricted fields, the limit may be two or three families. Do not be tempted by the very few exceptions or by the success syndrome, which says that bigger is better. The hard fact is that the percentage of ministry time given to evangelism per member decreases drastically in large, well-funded churches. Most "super churches" do almost no evangelism at all per member. (We must use the "per member" criteria to evaluate truthfully the effectiveness of a church's ministries.) The new members of a very large church usually are already Christians who were attracted from other smaller churches that could not compete with the expensive, more attractive programs.

Third, when a new church is planted near another church, generally both churches gain more new converts. They both gain even more new converts when they maintain biblical pastoral ethics and do not "steal sheep."

Finally, God blesses a mother church that makes the sacrifice (even weakening itself temporarily) to start a movement of daughter and granddaughter churches. Churches often resist reproducing daughter churches because they think it is too difficult. The truth is, once they become willing to make the sacrifice, it may be too easy! Missionaries with ample training and financial resources often hesitate to start a new church because they feel the need for even more money, education, or official backing. They are startled to see uneducated converts start churches without these advantages. The new believers, simply trusting the Holy Spirit to convert their friends in another neighborhood or town, disciple them in simple obedience--and a new church is born.

A church that gives a major part of its resources (time,

ministry, prayer, funds) to multiplying daughter churches will, in a generation, probably win from fifty to a hundred times as many people to Christ than it would if it concentrated all its energies inward. The multiplication is exponential, a chain reaction. It creates a movement of people for Christ such as has been witnessed all over the world where the pastors have let it happen with a sacrificial spirit, even to the point of begging their largest tithers and strongest worship leaders to go with a group starting a nearby daughter church.

130. Give missionary candidates experience in effective witnessing.

A sending church prepares its missionaries to witness for Jesus with the power of the Holy Spirit. This requires that they persevere in intercession for the unsaved, convinced of the power of the gospel to save those who hear it (Rom. 1:14-17). It also requires that they know and can readily communicate the essential gospel--the historical facts that one needs to know and act on to be saved, in any culture, stripped of all nonessentials (Luke 24:44-48; 1 Cor. 15:1-8).

A sending church is wise to plant daughter churches in other nearby communities and among local ethnic groups to provide this training for its foreign missionary teams and to fulfill the Great Commission in its own "Samaria" (Acts 1:8).

131. Seek cross-cultural apostles who are committed to go and multiply churches.

Church reproduction requires sacrifice, especially when it extends into pioneer areas held by Satan for centuries. A cross-bearing commitment is needed to give one's life to the discipling of an unreached nation (Luke 9:23, 57-62; see also 2 Tim. 2:1-13). A church should imitate the Antioch church, which sent out its first team (Paul, Barnabas, and John Mark) with prayer, fasting, and laying on of hands (Acts 13:1-3, 5). These modern apostles plan for the first new churches in a pioneer field to reproduce quickly, thus becoming mother churches.

132. List activities to help an established church reproduce.

To help an established church reproduce, develop an *Activity Review File* for it, together with your coworkers. This ARF might include the following examples of activities for mobilizing members of an established church for church multiplication:

✔ *Inform the entire body of its God-given task.*

Teach the entire church to obey Jesus' Great Commission, which is to disciple all nations.

✔ *Mobilize the entire body.*

Arrange for all members of the church (in all ministries, classes, departments, and groups) to pray and give for their missionaries and mission projects. Help them to be aware of the four areas where Jesus says we are to be witnesses: Jerusalem, Judea, Samaria, and the ends of the earth.

''Jerusalem'' corresponds to our own race and culture right where we live.

''Judea'' refers to people of our own culture in nearby communities.

''Samaria'' means peoples of other cultures nearby.

''The ends of the earth'' are distant, unreached peoples.

✔ *As a church, adopt an unreached people.*

Study unreached fields to adopt, pray for, and start churches among a presently unreached people.

✔ *Recruit workers for home and overseas ministry.*

Encourage all ages to consider mission service (challenge even the children so that God can be preparing them). Seek businessmen who can start or serve businesses that provide entrance and residence in otherwise inaccessible fields.

✔ *Train the workers.*

Involve missionary candidates in local cross-cultural church planting and personal discipling.

✔ *Send missionary teams.*

A church-based team might include members from like-minded sister churches. Team members remain accountable to their own church(es) to reproduce churches in the target field and to serve in a ministry that maximizes their spiritual gifts and natural strengths.

✔ *Commission missionaries for apostolic ministry.*

After prayer and fasting, lay hands on those that the Holy Spirit separates for foreign outreach (Acts 13:1-3).

✔ *Pray.*

Continually pray for the team and the people it serves.

✔ *Support the team.*

Keep giving sacrificially as the need arises.

✔ *Mobilize bi-vocational workers.*

Fields of restricted access need career ''tentmaker'' church planters who are experienced in cross-cultural church planting, especially small businessmen. Small businesses have been used most effectively to put church planters in touch with the responsive classes of people. Self-employment makes the missionaries believable with the local people. (If they see you hanging around without working, they wonder if you are with the CIA or something worse.)

An additional example of an ARF for a sending church (New Hope Community Church, Cucamonga, California) is given in Appendix D.

> **For help in leading your home church's mission efforts and planning long-range objectives for multiplication overseas, you might use the *Church Planter's Guide* and church multiplication materials (including pastoral training materials that allow for training on the job, especially in the third world), which can be obtained in English, Spanish, and other languages from Train and Multiply, Casilla 61, Viña Del Mar, Chile.**

133. **Mark items to review in appendix E. Write below general plans for your sending church(es):**

_____

_____

_____

_____

_____

_____

16. The Viewpoint of the Trainer of Pastors or Missionaries

134. To impart church multiplication skills, train pastors/elders and church planters *on the job*.

Recommended Bible Study: Acts 10:1-11:18. Look for guidelines for church planting and note a list of things that God, Cornelius, Peter, or Peter's team did to bring about the new church. You should find about ten things. Please do it before reading below.

Do you find the following?

Prayer, by both the church multiplier and the "man of peace" in the target field.

Receiving God's help to get over cultural prejudice.

Obeying the voice of God to go.

Serving as a team (not alone).

Contacting a "man of peace" (qualified contact: head of household and respected in the community).

Evangelizing where the "man of peace" is in control (being vulnerable).

Evangelizing a responsive person's entire network of family and friends.

Proclaiming the basic essential gospel account including the resurrection.

Letting the Holy Spirit convert the people (not pressuring them).

Baptizing without delay.

Spending time with them to further disciple the newly baptized converts.

Another recommended Bible Story: Acts 18:24-28. Look for how Apollos learned to teach the Word of God and the results.

Pastoral leaders are trained for church reproduction within the movement itself, in the churches. Patterson reports,

While coaching church planting teams in third world fields, I have found that many churches continue to send potential pastors away for training, only to find that few return--and the ones who do often fail to relate to their people and are the first to insist on the same unrealistic training policies for other pastors. They also fail to build the *Paul-Timothy* relationships with the leaders they do train, repeating their own "classroom only" experience. They also fail for the most part to use their gift of teaching in a way that mobilizes others for different gifts; the gifts of evangelist apostle (or cross-cultural church planter) and servant leader are consistently stifled by pastors whose training has only been in a traditional theological classroom. Training policies are not imported from another, more educated and affluent society!

To train new pastors/elders in a pioneer mission field for the kind of churches that multiply spontaneously, someone on our church planting team needs this skill. A church planting team in a pioneer field should have at least one permanent worker with the gift of teaching by discipling, who was also trained on the job.

Training on the wing's OK for lay leaders.

But to keep students' undivided attention in order to train *real* pastors, the Holy Dove needs an ivy covered campus separate from the churches.

You can't mean the One who flew down on Pentecost !!

Patterson explains how he came to recognize the need for discipling pastors on the job in a pioneer field:

Many times our new Honduran churches desperately needed pastors/elders. Discipling a new man on the job was slow. We had to arrange for a more experienced pastor or elder from an nearby church (who was often already overworked) to train him. He had to add another extension training center to his crowded itinerary or add the new man to his list of pastoral disciples (often a busy pastor or elder can disciple only two or three at this level, and it takes years). In our weaker moments we yielded to tradition and imported a pastor from the outside. These imported pastors had excellent Bible schooling--but no concept of discipling. They resisted training elders for a new daughter church with such words as: "Let's maintain things as they are. Let converts from other villages come listen to me preach!" (even if they had to walk thirteen miles). Or, "The few funds available will be spread too thin if we start more churches in the area!" Or, "We will lose control if these Paul-Timothy discipling chains extend beyond our own supervision!" Significantly, the only serious *doctrinal* problems we had were in churches pastored by these men. They and their congregations occasionally read the wrong books!

They stopped their churches from reproducing--every time. We had to fight the old battles all over again! We learned it the hard way: for church multiplication, train your pastors within the movement itself; do not import them.

Scoggins also relates his procedure for training leaders on the job:

One of the first responsibilities of our church planters is to seek out those men who are leaders, then mentor them in the skills of leadership. Usually the church planter teaches the basics of the Christian walk to this proto-leader, then helps him pass it on to another, newer believer. The church planter immediately sets up such discipleship chains from the moment there is more than one male believer (the same is done with women--older women teach the younger women). In this way leaders are trained in the art of shepherding by doing it, as opposed to studying it only out of books.

If we are starting a cluster of house churches in a new area and there is already another house church nearby, we will often use the leaders of the existing house church to train the emerging leaders in the new house churches. This way the churches develop strong relationships and much greater stability over the long term. In this way also we develop leaders on the job; more experienced leaders mentor newer ones, who begin at once mentoring even newer believers (the difference in spiritual age may be more one of character than actual duration of their faith).

135. To keep new churches multiplying where there are no experienced leaders, name *provisional* elders.

Paul found that he had to name relatively new believers as elders in the new churches in Galatia (Acts 14:23); church planters in *pioneer* fields often find this the case. Some call them "provisional" elders, meaning they are temporary or probational. Scripture warns not to lay hands suddenly on new leaders, that is, not to name someone to a position of pastoral leadership while he is still weak in his Christian life (1 Tim. 5:22). The practice of naming *provisional* elders applies to churches or fields with no experienced leaders available. It takes into account the spiritual maturity that God himself recognizes in persons whom the Holy Spirit has prepared even before they receive Christ. Cornelius is an example of such a person (Acts 10:1-15).

If you train pastors or elders for a new church, prepare an ARF that relates their pastoral studies to their shepherding activities. These activities are done by the church's members and led by their new local leaders. The elders of a new church in a pioneer field are discipled behind the scenes by a church planting team member or another worker of the target community. An ARF for a new church helps its new leaders to mobilize their own people; it might include the following activities:

✔ Call their people to repentance and faith;
✔ Baptize;
✔ Celebrate the Lord's Supper;
✔ Pray;
✔ Give;
✔ Worship;
✔ Teach the Word of God (including church history or doctrinal studies which help apply the Word);

✔ Love their neighbors in a practical way;

✔ Witness;

✔ Organize as elders;

✔ Form ministry and evangelistic groups;

✔ Authorize a treasurer to pay monthly expenses with a church budget;

✔ Reproduce daughter churches.

Etc.

136. Continually relate the doctrine (the Word of God) to the student's current practice (the work of God) as you teach.

Scripture requires that we combine the Word with our work. That is, we both hear and do the Word (Matt. 7:24-27; James 1:22-25). We also teach kingdom truth by integrating the old and the new (Matt. 13:52). We relate the practice and the theory not only as we talk about them but also as we assign reading that bears directly on what our people are doing in their ministry. We also relate theory and practice by assigning studies when they support an activity that the congregation or small group is beginning to do. Simply to teach the Word systematically to our people--without exercising the other spiritual gifts in the process--does not lend itself to church multiplication. Again, reading schedules for use in the home with practical questions are a great help here.

A list of *Helps for Combining Doctrine and Duty* is given at the end of this chapter.

137. Use formal residential theological education where conditions exist that warrant it.

Traditional seminary or Bible college training, especially when it includes practical internships, gives better results under the following circumstances:

✔ when there is a high level of education (uneducated students cannot assimilate the intensive study);

✔ when there is a high level of affluence (in poor areas the "elder" types who should train as pastors cannot leave their jobs, families, or fields, so the training institutions are attended by single young people, who often prove ineffective as pastors);

✔ when there are many well-established churches (unless students have a model of a well-organized church in mind and a concept of an experienced pastor, they cannot associate the theory they learn in the classroom with the areas of church life and pastoral work to which they apply).

Even where these three circumstances prevail we keep the *model* in mind. The pastors being trained are to serve as models for the flock, showing how to live a godly life. The congregation is to imitate them. Scoggins explains:

Pastors prepared in formal, resident seminaries often provide an effective model, but often they do not (especially if that is the only way they have been trained). Our experience with formally educated pastors shows that careful, personal shepherding still needs to occur in order for their pastoring to deal with more than theory. We have found that a low ratio of sheep to shepherds helps to maintain spiritual vitality. Jesus worked with a 12:1 ratio; our experience confirms this to be a practical proportion.

138. Use the gift of teaching to edify (build up) the church, not just to educate a student.

God requires that the gift of teaching, as other spiritual gifts, be used in certain ways.

First, we teach in love, to edify the body, to convert, to equip and lead, not just to teach the Word because of our love of teaching (Matt. 7.24-27; John 14:15; Eph. 4:11-16). The apostle makes it clear that no gift--including that of teaching as we train new pastors--justifies its own independent use as an end in itself.

Second, we use our teaching gift in harmony with the use of the other gifts given to the body united by the power of the Holy Spirit, and in an orderly way (1 Cor. 12:31-13:3; 14:26-40). Scoggins explains how his churches make sure that gifts are harmonized:

We have found that teaching must be done so that it equips the saint to do the work of the ministry (Eph. 4:11-12). We begin preparing our leaders with our vision statement for growth and reproduction. From there they figure out what equipping will be necessary to carry out the task. Reading schedules and teaching plans grow out of this evaluation. We emphasize that the goal of God is to extend his Kingdom; thus our teaching must be not only theoretical but also practical, applied to the building of the Kingdom.

Third, we teach in loving submission to the God-given shepherds of the church (Heb. 13:17). We teachers, perhaps more than most other types of ministers, must consciously and continually develop in humility the loving body life that harmonizes the exercise of the different gifts. This is especially true in training new pastors. Using gifts in specialized ministries or training institutions, if it means isolation from the rest of the body, destroys the very essence of what reproduces a church--a healthy church body that integrates gift-based ministries in love, through the Holy Spirit's power (Rom. 12:5; 1 Cor. 12:1-12, 18; Eph. 4:1-13).

139. To train pastors for multiplication, get the discipling skills you need for your particular field.

As you know by now, to train pastors in a restricted field you need the skill of training leaders by discipling them. In most churches, in fact, you will most effectively mobilize your people for action if you train evangelists, pastors, or church planters by personally discipling them. This discipling can be done as a supplement to regular classroom training. It can be done on the job in the field, in large or small groups or privately, as long as every worker receives the personal attention needed to become mobilized. By personal attention we mean that the discipler listens to the details of each student's practical work reports, teaches accordingly, plans with him, and holds him accountable to carry out the student's own plans.

140. Learn to disciple other leaders by *being* discipled.

If you do not have this experience, arrange to meet regularly with at least one adviser (preferably one who has mobilized other leaders for ministry while teaching them the Word of God). Do not try to learn reproductive discipling from books or lectures. While you are being discipled, you should also be discipling other potential leaders.

141. Use *Activity Review Files* to make the discipling of other leaders easier.

Using an ARF helps you to disciple evangelists, church planters, pastors or group leaders, wives of a church planters or businesspersons who facilitate the residence of a church planting team in a restricted field. As a discipler of leaders, you should meet regularly with

them and help them prepare and work their way through their own ARFs. You take personal responsibility for their effective ministry. They, in turn, may help you in your ministry. For example, you may be a pastor and may ask your disciple to help start a daughter church nearby.

Start recording your plans for how you will disciple, especially on the pastoral level. You may need to add new activities to your ARFs to accommodate your plans. Help those you disciple to develop their own personal ARF with their own list of goals and activity plans. Use it as an objective progress chart to guide them toward their own short-range and long-range plans (their God-given goals and life's objectives). Be ruthless in eliminating nice, spiritual-sounding activities and commitments that do not move them measurably toward their God-given goals.

In less sophisticated societies, where the need for a written Activity Review Chart is hard to grasp and appreciate, use a cultural equivalent of an ARF, something that amounts to a checklist of the national's plans. Patterson recalls:

Honduran leaders, especially the relatively uneducated village elders, hated paperwork. So we helped them to define their plans and job descriptions without it. They mentally listed things that a model person in the Bible did (Paul, Peter, David, or whoever had a ministry similar to that of the elder). Then they simply imitated the activities and virtues of the biblical person who was their example.

Wise church planters and leaders realize that God's call is to be faithful--not necessarily productive. Faithfully walking toward the goal is as important as achieving the goal, for it is the process that shapes and molds us. Someone has said, "God is more interested in the work he is doing in us than the work he is doing through us." Good works as seen by God proceed from a transformed heart and life. Thus family activities, which appear to have no direct relationship to your official church ministry, may indeed be far more important than this ministry, especially when a lonely wife or child comes to you asking you to do something with them.

If you still find it hard to prepare an ARF, ask for help to list your plans and activities. Seek a discipler who will meet with you regularly and help you monitor your progress as you plan the activities and pray with you as you and your people work through them.

142. Help your pastoral disciples to keep reproducing *other* disciples.

Recommended Bible Study: 2 Timothy 2:1-4. Look for principles and examples of reproductive discipling on the pastoral level.

If you train pastors, disciple only mature men (elders in the biblical sense, normally adult, serious heads of families), who will begin at once to help shepherd their own people. Elders are to be able to teach (1 Tim. 3:2); this gift enables them to train other pastors, who train still others (2 Tim. 2:2; 3:14-17). Scoggins reports:

We use a diagram based on 2 Timothy 2:2 to keep track of our discipleship chains. ("And the things that you have heard me say in the presence of many witnesses entrust to reliable men who will also be qualified to teach others.")

> Link 1: Missionary Paul teaches:
> Link 2: Timothy, his trainee, who teaches:
> Link 3: "Reliable men," who teach:
> Link 4: "Others."

We use these guidelines to construct discipleship chains; we keep track of the discipling relationships within the body and see how far the discipling is carrying down the chain. For multiplication-type growth, the chain must extend at least to the third link.

143. Help all who participate in the development of leaders to make the commitments needed for church multiplication.

Churches multiply when these *commitments* are made by the respective group or persons involved:

Churches: to begin quickly to reproduce daughter churches;

Pastors: to begin immediately to disciple their own "Timothies";

Pastoral trainees: as good "Timothies," to have a shepherding ministry while they study and to begin to disciple their own "Timothies" in the same pastoral training program (the first trainer in the chain focuses his attention on the second link in the 2 Tim. 2:2 discipleship chain);

Pastoral trainers: to require all their students to be active in a pastoral ministry (starting a church or group or helping to pastor a church) while they are studying to be pastors. Trainers continually relate the theory that they teach to their practical work, which requires <u>training on the job</u> while planting or developing the church, relating both theory and practice constantly, and <u>harmonizing the spiritual gifts</u>--including that of teaching new pastors--in a local, united, loving body.

All church leaders (pastors, elders, group leaders, evangelists, and trainees): to use biblical methods for personally discipling other new leaders.

144. Use biblical methods for discipling leaders.

If we conscientiously imitate Jesus and his apostles in the way we teach, we will do the following:

1. Require obedience, first and above all else, to Jesus' basic commands;

2. Train on the job while planting or developing the church, relating both theory and practice constantly;

3. Harmonize the spiritual gifts--including that of teaching the new pastors--in a local, united, loving body;

4. Foster loving relationships between teacher and disciple. The pastoral trainer takes personal responsibility for the effective ministry of his pastoral-level student and gives personal attention to the details of his ministry--almost a lost art in the United States today. The student should give something in return (encouragement, emotional support, or financial support). The teacher will also be open to receive as well as to give (Gal. 6:6), for his disciples need to give as well as receive. The Western concept that maturity means attaining independence is foreign to Scripture.

145. In each discipling session, *respond to your student's needs.*

This acronym *LEAP* lists what you must do in each discipling session:

*L*isten and plan: Listen to each disciple's reports (both progress and problems) and plans. Help him plan his field work for up to the next session. Keep a copy of the plans agreed upon, for the next session.

*E*valuate: Check on reading done (look over answers in workbooks or ask questions). Trainees may give a short message or summary of what they plan to teach their group; the adviser criticizes it constructively.

*A*ssign: Assign reading, in Scripture or other books, that corresponds to each trainee's immediate plans for his church, group, or personal disciples.

*P*ray: Each participant prays and is prayed for.

As you evaluate thier work and help them plan, role playing for dealing with field situations may be helpful. Cases involving confrontation, discipline, shepherding, and counseling can be walked through during the training session, before the disciples help others in a specific situation.

146. Require pastoral students to be active corporate disciples during their training by working in a pastoral ministry.

Require that each of your pastoral level trainees have a shepherding ministry while in training. He leads and disciples others, edifying in love his small group or congregation (Eph. 4:11-16).

147. Carefully relate reading to the practical work.

Assign reading in areas of Bible knowledge, doctrine, church history, and so forth that corresponds to a new activity that trainees are beginning with their people. List this reading in your ARF files under the corresponding activity. For example, when dealing with obedience to the commands of Christ, assign reading related to his deity, since Jesus relates obedience to his commands to his being all-powerful in heaven and on earth (Matt. 28:18-20). Or when assuring believers of God's grace, assign reading dealing with the doctrines of justification, the promise of eternal life, and Christ's present priestly intercession. Or when installing deacons to caring for the needy, assign reading related to the social duties of the church. If a specific chapter in a book does not relate to any practical ministry, it probably is not worth assigning, no matter how interesting or well written.

Verbal reports should be encouraged with all reading, in which trainees share how the reading applies to their family, church, and ministry. Verbal reports serve better than written reports for church planters or leaders to develop verbal skills in order to influence members of the flock. Advisers should become adept at asking questions that challenge trainees to grow in their ability to think and respond on their feet, as well as to reflect on the principles behind the church activities. (Why are we doing what we do? How does it tie into the big picture?)

148. Use materials that are geared to the trainees' level of education, to their needs, and to personal discipling.

Virtually all theological training programs started by Western missionaries (including Theological Education by Extension) are started on a level way too high for the students. Rather than use materials that are culturally irrelevant, write your own study outlines, or get studies that are written by persons experienced with third world pastoral training.

For a complete pastoral training curriculum based on personal discipling methods, useful for foreign fields where institutional training is impractical, contact *Train and Multiply*, Casilla 61, Via Del Mar, Chile.

For work in the United States or Canada, contact the *Fellowship of Church Planters*, 75 Capron Farm Drive, Warwick, RI 02886.

For help in developing a functionally ordered leadership training curriculum using discipling methods, read *Obedience Oriented Education*, available from *Church Planting International*, 9521-A Business Center Drive, Cucamonga, CA 91730.

149. Continually and ruthlessly evaluate the results of your teaching.

Evaluate your witnessing and teaching by results, not by your efforts. Help your students to measure their fieldwork progress in terms of converts baptized, changed lives, new churches and ministries, and so forth. If they are not getting the results you believe God wants them to have, change your methods of teaching. Help your adviser(s) to use your ARF to help you and your own disciples to monitor progress in both fieldwork and study.

Scoggins exhorts teachers:

Good teachers are brutal in their own self-evaluation as well as in listening to the input of others. Once an elder in one of our churches was complaining about his congregation. "I just preached one of the best messages of my life," he moaned, "but the congregation virtually slept through it!" He failed to make a brutal self-evaluation from the congregation's perspective.

150. Be creative in communicating God's Word.

Jesus and the Old Testament prophets used creative ways to communicate God's message. Try different methods of teaching. Do not overlook story telling, personal discipling, drama, dance, music, poetry, ritual, and symbolism. If working cross-culturally, avoid importing evangelism methods and curriculum from other cultures or from other social, educational, or economic levels. Keep exploring alternatives to methods that lack relevance--that is, methods that converts or workers cannot immediately imitate and pass on to others.

One form of story telling that is easy for most literate people is dramatic Bible reading. For Bible passages with dialogue, assign persons to stand and read the parts of the various participants in the conversation. They can mark their dialogue in their Bible beforehand. A narrator reads the portions that are not spoken as dialogue, skipping phrases such as "and he said." John 9, with voices of a narrator, a disciple, Christ, the Jews, the blind man, and the parents, provides a good example of a passage that can well be read dramatically.

151. Model all pastoral, evangelistic, and church planting skills as you train pastors.

Jesus commanded his disciples to do only what they had seen him do first, in a way they could imitate. As teachers of pastors/elders, we imitate Jesus' model if we want our discipling to be reproductive. For churches or

groups to reproduce spontaneously, do everything in a way that your students or disciples can imitate (1 Cor. 11:1). Model methods of teaching, preaching, discipling, leading worship, and using other skills in a way that new shepherds can imitate them; Jesus and Paul modeled all pastoral, evangelistic, and missionary skills that they expected their followers to use. Plan and arrange for leaders and elders to observe you or another discipler, doing the common pastoral or evangelistic duties.

Churches that train their own bi-vocational church planters by raising up daughter churches among the people of a different, nearby culture are more apt to start daughter churches that reproduce when their missionaries go overseas. They have the needed cross-cultural experience in starting new churches. Scoggins reports:

We found that little, portable paper booklets of from four to six separate studies that fit neatly inside a Bible are most practical. When we do a study with one person, we can give the booklet to that person and ask him or her to do the same study with another person. We found that we needed to develop methods of discipleship that were easily transferable and did not require a seasoned professional teacher or pastor. Discipleship is an art, and we improve our ability with practice. It's easy to become the "expert" that no one else can approach and everyone admires--but the result is that one person does all the discipling, and there is no reproduction.

Spiritual gifts helpful for teaching by modeling are wisdom, knowledge, leadership, exhortation, helps, and discernment.

152. Use equipment that is available to those who imitate your methods.

Avoid high-tech, expensive projectors, computers, or teaching tools if your people don't have them. In most fields we must discipline ourselves to avoid Western attitudes toward entertainment in worship, competition among pastors and churches, commercialism, professionalism, dependency on budgets, institutions, and technology.

153. If you need to hone the skill of discipling pastors, enlist one or more persons who are good models to disciple you.

If you do not yet have an adviser who is discipling you on the leadership level, arrange discipling with your pastor or another worker who loves you and will meet regularly with you (weekly, biweekly, or monthly). He should pray with you and counsel and help you to make your short- and long-range plans. Avoid advisers who try only to fit you into their own program or agenda. They must share your objectives. They do not need to be especially experienced in your field as long as they help you think through your short- and long-range plans and monitor your progress objectively using your own ARF. You may need two to four disciplers for different ministry areas.

154. Do not model skills or methods rooted in the paganism of your own culture.

Americans, for example, should not export to churches of other cultures an unbalanced emphasis on entertainment, worship of bigness, commercialization of church programs, purely academic pastoral training, and democratization of the Kingdom of Christ. These and many other Western cultural oddities stifle church reproduction wherever they are imported by culturally insensitive missionaries.

155. Develop personal, edifying, long-term relationships with your pastoral students.

Personal, balanced discipling motivates and mobilizes people for ministry more powerfully than using organizational pressure. It also provides a channel between a mother and daughter church through which the love and power of the Holy Spirit flows to help daughter churches to grow and develop. Remember, the important issue is not necessarily that our discipling is "one on one" (Jesus personally discipled twelve) but that we take personal responsibility for the details of our disciple's effective ministry. Scoggins cautions us:

Developing this relationship is like building a bridge. You want to build it strong, because someday it may have to bear the weight of a freight train driving across it! I once did a study on Jesus' interaction with his disciples. He spent three years working with them. But he saved much of his reproof and correction of them until the last week of his life. He built strong bridges that eventually did have to bear a tremendous amount of weight (e.g., see Matt. 16:21-23).

156. Supplement personal discipling with large group teaching when possible.

To meet in large groups saves time and encourages the participants--but we cannot do personal discipling if we only teach large classes. To do the kind of balanced discipling that mobilizes leaders for ministry, supplement large classes with small groups to give personal attention to details of individual ministry.

157. To deal with ministry details, separate disciples of different levels.

In small discipling groups for leaders, do not mix students of different social, economic, or educational levels if you sense that it stifles the initiative of the less educated or poorer workers (which commonly happens in developing countries).

158. Mark what applies to your ministry, among the following *Helps for Combining Doctrine and Duty:*

The following guidelines should help you relate your theoretical teaching with its practical application. Wise teachers and church leaders relate what they teach to the life of the Christian and of the church, as Jesus and his apostles did:

☐ **Help the new leaders of a church or group to envision what God wants the church to do in the future and then plan its activities; next, add the supporting theoretical studies to these activities.**

People of faith look ahead, focusing on where God is leading them and planning accordingly. Agree, in unified faith, on the potential of an obedient church to grow and reproduce, setting the corresponding God-given goals and planning the steps to reach them. Stagnant churches live in the past; their future plans are vague. Scoggins reports:

We encourage every church to have a written vision statement that has a specific reproductive goal with corresponding activities for evangelism and edification that will enable the group to achieve the goal.

☐ **Give priority to Jesus' basic commands.**

Arrange these activity plans in a logical, functional

order in the new church's ARF and add the biblical studies that correspond to them.

☐ **Add needed Bible study, doctrine, church history, pastoral work, and similar curriculum content to each activity in the list that they support.**

To prepare a functional curriculum, file ARF information in a functional order. In the church's ARF (not only in alphabetical order), file notes, commentaries, plans, references, and relevant passages in books and other sources under activities they support. Use the ARF both to guide the church in its activities and to relate the student's studies to the church and its development.

☐ **Monitor each new leader's progress with an ARF that corresponds to the ministry of that leader.**

Meet regularly with leaders to hear them report, plan, pray, advise, and evaluate their own progress.

☐ **Listen carefully to students' regular ministry reports and help them to make their own concrete, specific plans for immediate action.**

Teach Bible doctrine and other theological subjects in response to their church's immediate needs and opportunities. In each training session, let the communication flow two ways. Students report what their people are doing, and the teacher responds with counsel and biblical doctrine that applies immediately to the needs and opportunities facing the students' new church or group. Scoggins explains:

> As students progress in their understanding of ministry that leads to reproduction, they develop their own agenda for training. Normally this occurs at about the same time that they are reproducing themselves. As they develop another leader, they move one step back in the discipleship chain, actually replacing their mentor as the developer of leaders.

☐ **Model skills and activities in a way that the pastoral student can immediately imitate them.**

Model a skill (teaching, witnessing, celebrating the Lord's Supper, doing pastoral counseling, baptizing, disciplining, organizing the elders for their respective ministries, training small group leaders,

etc.). Then let your disciple do it in the liberty of the Holy Spirit. Scoggins relates:

> Problems will often appear at the behavioral level. We teach leaders that behavior is often only symptomatic of deeper problems at the motivational or affection level of the personality. We also teach pastors to be sensitive to motives rather than merely to behavior. Charles Spurgeon said that a preacher must change the affections of his congregation, not just their behavior. A good parent is not satisfied with a child whose behavior merely conforms to the code but desires one whose character (affections and motives) embraces the code. Jesus pointed out the source of sinful behavior--the heart. It is this heart that needs regeneration and then must go through the normal cycles of repentance and renewal.

☐ **Help the local leaders to plan ahead as you train them, and let them solve their own problems.**

Help them to define their long-range goals and to plan the little, easy-to-take steps leading up to them (like stepping stones across a shallow stream). Help them also to trust the Holy Spirit to plan and deal with obstacles, not to come running to you every time. Do not fear that you will lose control. You are more apt to lose control of those whose liberty you limit.

To help new leaders plan for reproduction, remember the illustration in chapter 7 above of a grain of corn or rice. Point out that we cannot make it grow; we only sow, water, and cultivate it in faith; God gives the growth (1 Cor. 3:6). Then calculate what happens if we let one grain reach its miraculous potential (as Jesus said, a hundredfold); in just a few years of such reproduction we could feed the entire human race. This is the way Jesus said his church would grow and reproduce. Every time we look at the grass and trees or eat virtually anything, we are enjoying the fruit of God's miraculous reproductive power; all creation reminds us daily of how our Father makes every living thing reproduce! But when it comes to reproducing his body on earth, he limits his infinite power to our weak faith. We ask him, constantly, to do it.

☐ Teach new pastors/elders to solve the root causes rather than the symptoms of their own churches' problems, and to discern the difference.

Patterson relates the following example:

A devout Honduran pastor was disturbed because the señoritas in his church kept running off to live in "common law marriage" (i.e., without the blessing of church or state). He failed to discern the real cause, which was poverty and despair. In his area the girls of marriageable age were underfed, unwanted, and miserable in the little village huts they shared with their oversized families, and they saw no hope for a better future. So he preached incessantly against the sin of fornication. The girls, however, were not motivated by sex.

Such preaching, however, merely kept the idea of a possible way of escape from their plight before their minds. As a result, his church had more cases of such fornication than other churches in the area.

☐ Do not so fear false doctrine or bad practices creeping in that you chain leaders to your own rules and policies.

Rules growing out of fear almost always stifle spontaneous growth and development. It also causes a subtly rebellious spirit that eventually opens the door to the very errors we fear. Every time we make rules that have no explicit basis in Scripture, we will sooner or later encounter circumstances in which they limit the free working of the Holy Spirit.

Scoggins relates an interesting incident:

We have found that a group of leaders meeting together will often see more clearly the issues involved than an outsider. (Church planters, unless they live permanently in the community and plan to stay in the church, are outsiders!) In one of our churches a woman wanted to join who was already a believer. She had come to Christ years ago while reading the Bible with her teenage girlfriend. After reading that they should be baptized, they went down to a nearby quarry and baptized each other! Was the baptism valid? The group debated for hours. Was baptism done only by the church, or are private baptisms valid in unusual circumstances? Can women baptize?

Can non-ordained people baptize? They discussed the mode of baptism (sprinkling versus immersion) as well as the number of immersions (one of the brothers had come from a church that immerses three times forward) and infant baptism.

It was fascinating to watch these men, who were untrained by human institutions, deal with the issue by turning to the Scriptures. They finally agreed that if it was done from a heart pure with the desire to be obedient, then it was probably acceptable to God and would be acceptable by the fellowship of house churches. They thought it through with no input from church planters or traditionally trained pastors. I was impressed with how fully they explored the issue and with the effect on the congregation. I have been to many ordination counsels and can't remember such a thorough illumination of this issue in its practical import.

Patterson also recalls:

A devout Roman Catholic girl and her boyfriend were attacked by a shark while swimming off the coast near where we lived. She dragged him ashore and saw that he had only moments to live, since he was losing blood from several large gashes. She took seawater and baptized him in the name of the Father, Son, and Holy Spirit. Many questioned its validity. The bishop declared the baptism to be valid, however, even though not done by the church or by an ordained pastor. The girl, who believed that she was led by the Holy Spirit, felt the freedom to do it and was not inhibited by tradition as many Evangelicals and Catholics would have been.

☐ **Write or get textbooks that are geared to the local, present needs and educational level of your group or congregation.**

Texts written even by inexperienced missionaries are far more effective, if prepared for a specific people's needs and on their reading comprehension level, than the best texts if written for another time or culture. Scoggins explains:

We have found it very helpful to put together little pastoral-level study booklets that deal with

Scripture passages on a particular, currently needed topic. These booklets are set up as daily reading schedules; each week focuses on a specific sub-theme of the topic. It starts with a question, with seven days of reading, each day focusing on a passage or two. For instance, we have a booklet on spiritual warfare. Each of five weeks focuses on a related theme:

The reality of the War;
Focus of the War (the Church);
The Enemy;
Schemes of the Devil; and
Agents of the Evil One.

We have developed many such booklets as they have been needed for the life and development of the churches.

☐ **Mobilize many, if not all, of a church's members for ministry.**

Normally, it is far easier to mobilize a church's members if the church is small. Take advantage of a new church's small size to set the precedent for its future work: mobilize all its members for ministry while they are still pliable. Scoggins relates:

One of the study booklets we have created is called *Finding Your Place in the Body*. Once a person has been shepherded into the body and understands that we "have been saved to serve" (Gal. 5:13), we use this booklet with them to study spiritual gifts and their application in the body. We use this study in conjunction with the vision statement to help new believers to pray and seek how God has equipped them to help the body attain its vision. This reinforces the ongoing teaching that the church is a community of people who have been given something by God to be passed on to someone else.

When a church reaches an unwieldy size (i.e., too large to effectively mobilize most of its members), we reorganize. The congregation should either separate members to start a daughter church nearby or form small ministry groups or sub-congregations where members can be mobilized to help give pastoral care to each other on a personal and family level. Scoggins states: "We have found that small ministry group size

is ideal at from eight to twelve members. Some groups may exist more for outreach and others for edification."

☐ **To mobilize leaders for church reproduction, we orient their training (even that of serious, intelligent, highly motivated, mature leaders) to loving obedience.**

The key to combining learning with obedience is to establish first the foundation of loving obedience. Obedience comes before discernment (John 7:17). If we teach heavy Bible doctrine before one has learned simple, loving, childlike obedience, we stifle that person's discipleship.

Scoggins relates:

We have observed that maturity comes from practiced obedience (Heb. 5:12-14). We try to avoid the paralysis that arises from teaching heavy Bible doctrine to potential leaders before they can apply it and learn to live in simple, loving, childlike obedience. Our Western, seminary model for developing leaders tries to prepare them for every contingency; in the process, the theological student sometimes gets the idea that professional proficiency comes from ever-higher learning rather than on going to the Master. This is in contrast to the on-the-job training Jesus gave his disciples. He sent his apprentices out (where they often failed) and evaluated their learning of both doctrine and pastoral skills as they worked. In Jesus' model, leaders learn by doing and studying (always related) rather than by theoretical instruction in the doctrines of the faith in a classroom only. Paul's attitude toward his own teaching echoes this approach; he acknowledged that it was to be evaluated only by the lives and work of those he trained (1 Cor. 3:1-9; 2 Cor. 3:1-6).

Leaders often seek more training from us because of a feeling of inadequacy. Before doing detailed doctrinal training (as important as that is), we train them first to depend upon the Lord. Having been exposed to many seminary-trained leaders, I have noticed with interest a tendency by many of them to rely upon their books and theologians, rather than upon *the* book and its Author.

In rapid reproduction of churches, traditional seminaries cannot keep pace with the need for leaders, especially for lay elders. Also, seminary-trained leaders seldom have the flexibility to disciple leaders on the job, keeping up with the moving of the Spirit. They tend to train others the way they were trained. I myself was trained within a church in a personal discipleship relationship and therefore rely upon this method. The seminary-trained men I have met pretty much insist that such training is inadequate. They encourage men in their churches who are called to the ministry to go away to seminary, thus failing to train the large numbers of elders at the time they are needed to shepherd truly reproducing churches.

☐ **Keep gearing the training—week by week and month by month—to current needs and opportunities.**

Patterson relates an experience that underlines how missionaries often overeducate new pastors/elders:

A Honduran pastor who had been extensively educated in Guatemala heard about the little comic books we developed to teach serious theology on a pastoral level for less-educated people. He asked for some of these training booklets, explaining, ''In seminary I learned wonderful things from the Word of God. The only problem is, having returned to my church of semi-literate peasants, I find I can no longer communicate to them.'' He read a few of our booklets and later wrote, ''This is what I want. Send me the rest.'' Later he thanked us for helping him get back on the same cultural wavelength as his own people.

Many churches stagnate in their growth because they fail to integrate the Word and the work of God. Traditional pastoral trainers often follow only the training model they know best--the traditional classroom. They emphasize learning more and more doctrine, without practicing the ministries and commands of God that correspond to the teaching. But disciplers avoid creating ''hearers only'' by being and training doers of the Word (James 1:22). Beware of teachers who teach theory only, without enabling their students to

apply it immediately. This numbs the discipling process and makes the mobilization of church members in ministry very difficult. The imbalance of weighing too heavily on the side of the academic is contagious and sidetracks sincere workers who fear they cannot serve until they learn a lot more. Let them learn and serve at the same time, as the disciples of Jesus and Paul did. This kind of training brings with it true humility, since those being trained rely not upon their own previous learning but upon the Spirit of God at work in the church, the body of Christ.

☐ **Mobilize non-academic pastors for uneducated people groups and subcultures.**

The working classes of the world need thousands of non-academic lay pastors who are trained on the job. Churches among the poor and uneducated thrive and reproduce with non-academic pastors and elders, trained on the job by godly pastors. But these churches almost always lose power when they depend on outside institutions to train their pastors. A similar problem would develop if all the soldiers in a campaign were prepared by West Point--all generals and no riflemen. We need both, but in a sane proportion (perhaps one academic pastor for every twelve non-academic pastors?). In most pioneer fields the need is best met by training new pastors/elders by extension education--if it uses biblical discipling principles. Scoggins affirms:

In Rhode Island our house churches have relied on this type of man. We have men who have been ordained who have never attended college and some who didn't even finish high school. We even have one or two who never entered high school. But they are good shepherds, seasoned by experience in the world, who love the Lord and his people.

159. Remember to mark items by their numbers in Appendix E, that you plan to follow up on.

Also, file detailed training plans in your ARFs, while they are still warm. You might also see Appendix B which gives an example of an ARF with *Activities for New Churches*, to help you relate pastoral training curriculum to what the churches are doing.

17. The Viewpoint of the Church Leader

First, make sure your own flock grows bigger and bigger.

That's *something to crow about--success!!*

Don't let your chicks even *think* of building another nest of their own !!

<u>Recommended Bible Studies: 1 & 2 Timothy.</u> Look for things that pastors/elders do with their people.

160. For best results in reproductive discipling, mobilize every member--young and old--of your congregation for gift-based ministry.

We may have various ideas about how to measure the health of our church. Ephesians 4:15-16 makes it clear, however, that its health depends on the "proper working of each individual part." This is not an unattainable ideal, as some assume, if we practice balanced, obedience-oriented discipling. If we emphasize coming to church only to get one's needs met, we will have few sacrificial workers. Let us imitate the example of Jesus' and his apostles, who called all who entered the Kingdom of Christ to a life of unselfish, cross-bearing service (see Gal. 5:13; Heb. 9:14). Scoggins observes:

Discipleship, or following Christ in service in his Kingdom in such a way that we become like him, is progressive. Some respond immediately and make rapid progress, entering quickly into service. We have seen progress so rapid that a man has gone from being saved to being a leader in less than a year. Obviously, God has been preparing such persons for service in his Kingdom even before they were saved. Praise God for such Kingdom people!

But others bring with them many scars from this world, which are healed through illumination by the Holy Spirit, repentance, and renewing of the mind. These stumble forward with fits and stops and require much healing before they can contribute significantly to the Kingdom. But even during this crippled stage they can be serving in some way; their contribution should be recognized and appreciated. They can pray for the leaders and the needs of the body and often will have words of encouragement for the downhearted. Some of their healing will come as they contribute their part in the kingdom.

I have a retarded brother who, despite his mental handicaps, has been quite a challenge to me. One day he asked me who would preach the gospel to people like himself? His concern challenged me. Children who know Christ also need to see themselves as contributors to the Kingdom. A Jewish boy in Jesus' times was considered a man at age twelve and was expected to carry out his religious duties in the synagogue. We often have no place for children to serve until after they graduate from college! Maybe that's why we lose so many. They do not see service in God's Kingdom as a part of their life. Instead church is a place where they are entertained and served. When the world offers better entertainment and more attractive opportunities to do things, they are seduced.

In our house churches we sometimes have "affirmation meetings," where members of the congregation mention how they have seen others minister in the body. This encouragement helps spur others to greater ministry. Little teaching is done at such meetings, but the ministry of helps, encouragement, reproof, and compassion are made more visible; otherwise they often go unnoticed.

All of us ought to be progressing measurably in our walk with the Lord. Those who are not need to recognize that something is wrong. If our children stop growing, we take them to see a doctor; likewise those who have experienced new life in Christ ought to keep growing. We cannot accept "nominal" growth as normal in a reproducing church. We need to detect and oppose the "convenience volunteer" mentality when we mobilize our people for ministry ("I will do ministry when it is convenient--when it is not, I have my own things to worry about"). In God's army there are no such convenience volunteers, only conscripts. Unlike the volunteer militia in the beginning of the American Revolutionary War who went home when the going got tough, we are "regulars" who have been drafted for the duration of the war. For us there is no turning back! Those who will not move forward need our help in order to remove Satan's barriers. Scoggins explains how they correct these who continue to resist sacrificial service:

We help them to see that the church is like a big boat pulling away from the dock. You either get on, or you will be left behind by your own choice. Some churches hesitate at the dock while timid members make countless excuses for not getting on. Eventually even the most committed grow weary waiting for their brothers to make up their minds, and join the uncommitted standing on the dock watching the boats go by.

Disciples who show progress need to be encouraged to go forward and given more responsible ministry, on the principle that "he who is faithful in little will also be faithful with much" (Luke 19:17). We include them in our meetings when we initiate ministry, plan, and set objectives so that they feel that they are "in" and not simply subordinate to the elders and paid staff.

Especially in Western cultures, many larger churches find it hard, often impossible, to turn over key positions to lay workers. One hears the complaint frequently, "But you cannot count on them." Yet other large churches have an abundance of accountable volunteer workers. Why the difference? When we examine the churches with many reliable lay workers, we find that their leaders do not hesitate to challenge members to loving, childlike obedience to Christ. They are not polarized into a paid staff who are accountable versus the others who attend church to get their needs met (then give offerings in return, paying the staff to do the real work).

161. First determine what God wants your people to do; only then organize for it.

Let organization grow out of a thorough understanding of what God wants you to do (do not attempt to inject new plans into an organizational structure originally set up to carry out other, different plans). Remember, a pastor who is not mindful of the specific activities that God wants his people to do in the future cannot lead; he can only teach.

Here are some commonly encountered enemies of reproductive organization:

- ✔ outmoded methods and organizational structure;
- ✔ overcontrol;
- ✔ delegating with too many safeguards (rules, policies);
- ✔ building the work around the organization (rather than building the organization around the work);
- ✔ placing a new cluster of highly reproductive house churches under the leadership of a traditional regional church board (instead of overseers that understand church reproduction and are highly motivated to continue it);
- ✔ failure to maintain relationships with members who leave a church or group to start another.

The last "enemy" above is especially important for wives and teenagers, who are usually more motivated by relationships than by the vision for reproducing new churches or groups. The relationships might be maintained with an occasional celebration or fellowship for members of all churches or groups and by arranging personal discipling of the leaders of the new group or church by the leaders of the parent group or church. Mobilize the older women to disciple the younger women or those newer in the faith in the new churches or groups (Titus 2:3-4).

Scoggins reports:

We have found that house churches can reproduce more rapidly, thus requiring regular changes in organization and relationship building. Monthly meetings that include members of the entire network of churches help to keep up old relationships. In addition to monthly meeting of all the churches, we also have weekly men's prayer meetings, women's meetings, and youth meetings. Discipleship chains often extend from one church to another, especially when a new house church begins.

Organizing for normal, spontaneous reproduction requires flexible, open-ended organization (in which churches or groups are free and encouraged to reproduce themselves, without being tied to rules imposed by a controlling board or grandmother church). Each church is a "whole new ball game," entitled to make its own rules for its own ministry--and to make its own mistakes. The best organizational structures for the multiplication and continued fellowship of churches and groups grow normally out of the loving relationships already developing in the process of training assistant pastors/elders in the churches or groups.

162. Review the ministries of your church(es) periodically to verify continued practice of those things that are essential.

Wise leaders regularly review and evaluate progress in all vital ministries. Examples of essential church ministries are listed in *Appendix B*. The ministries done by your church(es), like all ministries in the New Testament, should grow out of Jesus' commands. Here we list his commands with some of the corresponding ministries:

Command	Corresponding Ministries
Repent, believe and be baptized	Evangelism
Pray	Prayer, intercession, worship
Love, forgive	Fellowship, pastoral administration, organization and church life, family care, mercy ministries
Break bread	Worship
Give	Stewardship, mercy ministries
Make disciples	Teaching, spiritual life, pastoral care and counseling, biblical doctrine, foreign missions, training pastors/elders and missionaries, daughter churches, regular progress review

If a church or Christian organization does not allow you or your disciples to obey Jesus' specific commands before all else in your ministry, pray for a change. In the Great Commission, Jesus based this obedience on his deity (Matt. 28:18-20). No person or organization has higher authority; you cannot be his fully committed disciple if you yield first to conflicting policies from another source. Facing this very situation in his trial for heresy, Martin Luther risked being burned at the stake as he answered before the emperor, "I cannot go against my conscience, since to do so is neither safe nor right."

163. Mark the numbers in *Appendix E* by item headings that you wish to follow up.

If you are a leader in your church, together with the other leaders list detailed ministry plans for your church in your ARFs. Also, *Appendix D* contains an ARF with activities for a *sending church*. List below your general plans for your church as a body:

_____

_____

_____

_____

_____

_____

_____

_____

_____

_____

_____

_____

_____

_____

_____

_____

Aw, c'mon,
don't take this
stuff so seriously.

18. The Viewpoint of the Mission Career Counselor

If you fly close with the Holy Dove you don't need no human counselors.

Then why did the Lord establish pastors and elders ??

Recommended Bible Story: Jonah. Look for good or bad examples of attitudes that a missionary career counselor should help those he counsels to acquire.

164. Provide *unbiased* career counseling.

Churches, schools and mission agencies should give counseling that is unbiased so that the Holy Spirit can guide new workers with freedom. Otherwise, missionaries and agencies will continue the present unbalance in their global outreach, neglecting needed ministries and fields by clustering missionaries where there is already an unbalanced concentration of efforts.

A wise, unbiased career counselor bears in mind all areas of mission activity, from the local sending church to the farthest unreached field, in order to counsel effectively and objectively. This need for unbiased, comprehensive counseling becomes increasingly evident as we listen to complaints from those who received missionary counseling from recruiters for mission agencies or training institutions. Although these recruiters mean well, their counsel is usually biased (they unconsciously recruit for their own organization, field, or type of ministry, which may be inconsistent with a person's calling and gifts). The family and career disasters that result are heartbreaking.

165. Keep reviewing your church's mission work.

Mission counselors in a local church should review their own church's missionary outreach at least once a year, to monitor its progress and recommend needy areas to local workers. Keep in mind the entire scope of mission mobilization. Look over the following fourteen missionary mobilization steps to see that your church, its missionaries, and the agencies it works with are touching essential bases. To disciple all peoples as Jesus commands, missionary decision makers, curriculum developers, and career counselors deal with the following fourteen sets of persons, each of which represents a step in the process of mission mobilization.

The mobilization steps listed below are reviewed in *backward order*. It helps to start with our final objective, then reason back step by step, to what has to be done first. For example, we first focus on our final objectives and the realities of the target field. Then we can better plan the intermediate steps to deal with it, especially on the team preparation. Finally, after we know what kind of team we need, we are ready to sharpen the vision and methods of those who work at home to send the team.

On the field
14. National church mobilized
13. Regional leaders mobilized
12. National churches mobilized
11. National pastors trained and mobilized
10. New Christians discipled
9. Pre-Christians evangelized

During team formation
8. Transferable methods adapted
7. Two-thirds world churches mobilized
6. Bi-vocational workers engaged

At the home base
5. Missionaries trained
4. Missionary trainers mobilized
3. Mission agencies mobilized
2. Sending churches mobilized
1. Career counselors mobilized

166. Help leaders of a sending church to plan and arrange for needed *training and orientation*.

If you mobilize persons or groups in a home or sending church, consider these activities (mark those you plan to deal with later):

☐ Train potential missionaries. Missionaries, including Bi-vocational workers and workers from two-thirds world churches with whom we partner, need special training. If they work in a restricted field, they need:

> **vocational skills** or apprenticeships in small businesses;

> **discipling skills** to train pastors/elders in the Word on the job;

> **evangelism skills** for low-profile, incarnational discipling of pre- and new Christians; and

> **worship skills** for small house churches.

Missionaries from two-thirds world churches should be trained where they are, or in their target field. They definitely should not be trained in a third, Western culture, especially if it moves them into a higher economic bracket from those with whom they will work. This cancels the advantage they would otherwise normally have of being culturally closer to their target field than Western missionaries.

☐ Mobilize trainers of missionaries. Most missionary trainers need much more experience in the discipling skills required now in the remaining unreached fields. These skills include reproducing house churches cross-culturally and training leaders by discipling them on the job and from behind the scenes. They also need to know how to deal with two-thirds world workers and cross-cultural entrepreneurs.

☐ Explain to your church how to prepare and send church planting teams. Starting with the main pastor, the leaders of a church should plan together for the church body to adopt and disciple an unreached people.

☐ Help mission agencies to send teams with the needed pastoral and vocational skills. For many of the remaining unreached fields, mission agency administrators must integrate small business managers, entrepreneurs, disciplers of pastors and workers from the two-thirds world on the same team, in close cooperation with sending churches.

For help in career guidance technique, use the *Perspectives Ministry Career Guide*, available from William Carey Bookstore, 1605 Elizabeth, Pasadena, CA 91104.

167. Mobilize people for these ministries through their love for Jesus.

Make sure a person is serving out of their desire to obey Christ--not because of your organizational authority. If they aim to serve overseas, make sure their commitment is to do simply what Jesus says, not to a team or a term of service, etc. *Appendix D* contains an example of a detailed ARF with activities for a sending church. *Appendix A* contains an example of a personal ARF (what a person himself, or his family, plans to do).

178. Mark items by their numbers in *Appendix E*, to follow up. Also file detailed plans in your ARFs, while they are still warm, to mobilize a sending church. Note your general plans below:

_____

_____

_____

_____

_____

_____

_____

_____

_____

_____

APPENDIX A. An Example of a
Personal *Activity Review File:*

Confirm my commitment with prayer and consultation with my wife and pastor.
    Date begun_____ Done_____

Define specifically the type of ministry that I will do (do another *Spiritual Gifts Inventory*).
    Date begun_____ Done_____

Discuss my wife's role in ministry with her, come to an agreement.
    Date begun_____ Done_____

Determine if we can join or form a church based team from our own church (read George Miley's *Antioch Network papers*)
    Date begun_____ Done_____

Determine with which mission agency and team we will serve (read *Perspectives Ministry Career Guide*, section E).
    Date begun_____ Done_____

Investigate the people groups in northwestern Vietnam and select the one which will be most likely to respond, and where our team can work with an export business.
    Date begun_____ Done_____

Get Lowell to disciple me and mentor me as I learn (and teach) the books of Genesis and Exodus to my small group.
    Date begun_____ Done_____

Get practice in training small group leaders by apprenticing Fred and Sam in my small group; help them form their own groups (read Logan's *Beyond Church Growth*, also Neighbor's book on cell groups).
    Date begun_____ Done_____

Practice more "incarnational evangelism" (especially with heads of families; use T&M's *Best News* series of stories).
    Date begun_____ Done_____

Do an internship with a businessman who is already exporting from S.E. Asia (read Patterson's *Missionary Businessperson's Manual*).
    Date begun_____ Done_____

Pay off my college loan.
    Date begun_____ Done_____

Start learning the language; get tapes from Victor.
    Date begun_____ Done_____

Get Nancy's teeth straightened.
    Date begun_____ Done_____

Get on a family health plan.
    Date begun_____ Done_____

Help Mom and Dad to accept, emotionally, my call overseas.
    Date begun_____ Done_____

APPENDIX B. An Example of *an Activity Review File* for A New Church

Three levels for each ministry are listed: *beginning*, *growth* (i.e., ongoing ministry), and *reproduction* (advanced). Do not try to begin all three levels of a ministry one after another; after developing a ministry on one level, go to another ministry and return later to the first at a more advanced level. Note that although the reproduction level is listed last, God may do it any time for any ministry; be ready to move with him.

Disciple

Beginning level: You and your disciples learn and do all of Jesus' basic commands (review the Gospels)

Growth level: Leaders disciple newer leaders, including those for daughter churches and new cell groups (read Scoggins, *Church Planters' Fellowship Manual*).

Reproduction level: Pastoral trainees (new elders) take on pastoral responsibility in new churches or groups--be ready for God to do this any time (read Patterson's *Church Planting through Obedience Oriented Teaching*).

Pray

All levels: You and your disciples pray and praise God daily. (Use Spurgeon's *Morning and Evening Devotions*).

Evangelize

Beginning level: All members witness to friends and relatives; converts are baptized (read Acts).

Growth level: The church sends out teams to evangelize.

Reproduction level: Leaders help daughter churches mobilize evangelistic teams (inductive studies: Acts 2:36-47; 10 and 13-14).

Worship

Beginning level: All churches celebrate the Lord's Supper.

Growth and reproduction levels: Congregations practice all essentials of corporate worship (praise, confession and assurance of forgiveness, application of the Word, Eucharist, prayer, giving, fellowship) and celebrate sacred seasons of the church year (Read Schmemann, *The Eucharist*).

Practice fellowship

Beginning and growth levels: All members cultivate loving fellowship, forgiving and asking forgiveness for all offenses, building all organization on loving relationships (do a topical study on passages dealing with love, unity and fellowship).

Reproduction level: Each church or group as a body maintains loving, cooperative interchurch (inter-group) relationships, including regular united celebrations with sister churches or groups.

Shepherd

Beginning and growth levels: Teachers help parents and new teachers to relate Bible stories (historical events) dealing with vital doctrines, common personal, family, and church needs; counselors lovingly, patiently, and humbly correct--without condemning--those with personal or family problems (read Adams, *Effective Leadership* and Anderson's *The Bondage Breaker*).

Reproduction level: Small group leaders train assistant group leaders, who form new groups

Reproduce daughter churches

Beginning level: Pastors/elders disciple new pastors/elders for new churches (finish Logan/Rast, *Church Planter's Workbook* and read T&M's *Church Planter's Guide*).

Growth and reproduction levels: Mother churches (groups) mobilize daughter churches and new groups to multiply (help daughter churches to start granddaughter churches, etc.).

Teach to edify

Beginning level: Teachers and pastors teach in a way that their disciples imitate them.

Growth level: Church members do inductive Bible studies to interpret correctly and apply God's Word to their lives and ministries.

Reproduction level: Teachers prepare assistants on the job as new Bible teachers for new small groups and daughter churches.

Grow in Christ

Beginning level: All members cultivate the hope that purifies, to live the new life in Christ.

Growth and reproduction levels: Leaders discern the daily guidance of the Holy Spirit; family heads shepherd their families to help them grow in Christ (Use CPI's *Bible Readings*).

Practice Christian stewardship

Beginning level: All members give in faith, expecting our Father's heavenly reward.

Growth level: Elders discern worthy projects and persons to support, channeling giving through the church, and develop a church budget (do a topical study on giving).

Reproduction level: All give sacrificially to start other churches at home and abroad.

Organize

Beginning level: Elders integrate different ministries in one loving, united body.

Growth level: Small group leaders and new church elders provide total pastoral care (read Neighbor's books)

Reproduction level: Small groups multiply themselves and their ministries in both mother and daughter churches.

Mobilize for global outreach

Beginning level: Pastors/elders help each church as a body to discern and pray for unreached fields.

Growth level: Churches recruit and prepare missionary teams.

Reproduction level: Churches send teams to start churches in ripe, unreached fields (Use the *Perspectives Ministry Career Guide*).

Strengthen families

Beginning level: Families develop loving communication between spouses and children (write for the *Focus on the Family* materials).

Growth and reproduction levels: Parents practice loving Christian discipline in the home; elders and older Christian women counsel spouses, couples, or children with problems and help fathers to shepherd their own families.

Serve the needy

Beginning level: The church body and its members obey Jesus' Great Command to love our neighbor in a practical way.

Growth level: Deacons/deaconesses develop ministries involving many or all members to help the sick and needy (read Paddock, *We Don't Know How* and survey two projects in which church planting is being successfully integrated with community development).

Reproduction level: Churches or groups alleviate injustice and poverty in other communities and fields (especially through daughter churches started there).

Appendix C. An Activity Review File for a Church Multiplication *Team*

If you lead or supervise a church planting team, you may find your job much easier if your team's Activity Review File includes the following activities for team members. Mark items that you plan to give special attention:

ACTIVITIES FOR STARTING A NEW CHURCH

☐ **Prayerfully select and focus on the specific people you plan to disciple.** Study a people group to determine the most responsive segment (normally, the working class) of the people group.

☐ **Target people who are culturally similar to you and your team members.** *Or* add to your team church planters from other fields that are culturally closer to the target people--especially during those first months or years when all evangelism must be done by outsiders. Remember--church multiplication is delayed for many years by making too large a cultural leap. If your church "adopts" an unreached people and prays for it, God will give members the apostolic gift to disciple the people.

☐ **Recruit team members committed to seeing the job through.** Remember, they commit simply to do what Jesus says, to disciple a people group no matter how long it takes or what sacrifice is required. If your church is small, cooperate with sister churches to form an apostolic team.

☐ **Bond with those you have chosen.** Identify socially with the people of one community--not with a missionary compound, other missionaries, or foreigners.

☐ **Bind Satan.** Pray in Jesus' all-powerful name to bind Satan and his demons in your targeted area. Remember, they were defeated totally by the cross and the resurrection of Jesus Christ. They have no real power, except in the lies that people are willing to belie*ve.*

☐ **Filter out nonessentials.** Avoid nontransferable methods, attitudes, and equipment--including the ways you teach and worship.

☐ **Take advantage of the brutal class discrimination in most resistant fields as you target the most responsive segment of your chosen people group** (but avoid messy foreign politics). For the initial penetration of highly restricted areas, seek to live among people who desperately want change, who do not defend the *status quo*. Also, seek to live where authorities do not watch closely.

☐ **Maintain constant, fervent prayer for the unsaved and for converts.**

☐ **Seek good contacts.** Look first to responsive heads of families, preferably friends or relatives of believers.

☐ **Witness for Jesus.** Begin with heads of households. Help unsaved heads of families repeat to their families Bible stories that show the value of Jesus' death (forgiveness) and resurrection (holy, eternal life).

☐ **Baptize.** Baptize entire families as soon as possible, as the apostles did.

☐ **Break bread.** Celebrate the Lord's Supper with the new believers in weekly worship--on their "turf."

☐ **Teach.** Teach the new believers to obey the commands of Jesus and apply the Word of God to their lives.

☐ **Organize.** Name, train, and mobilize the new elders for their different ministries (Acts 14:23).

☐ **Agree on each leader's wife's ministry** (on the team and among the new pastors/elders). Talk it over again when there is a change in her status such as children born or grown into a less dependent stage of development, etc.

☐ **Keep doing evangelism in the community**--especially after starting public worship services.

☐ **Make worship an edifying celebration.** Prepare well, ahead of time, even for a tiny group.

☐ **Give responsibility to the local leaders and avoid overcontrol or subsidizing by outsiders.**

☐ **Arrange for clear, regular accountability for everybody.**

☐ **Disciple new leaders as Jesus and His Apostles modeled it.** Do not send them out of their own community to receive pastoral training. Disciple them from behind the scenes, on the job.

THE SEPARATION CEREMONY

☐ **Launch a team for a distant field with a serious *separation ceremony.*** Separate the church planters through the power of the Holy Spirit, as in Acts 13:1-3. This assures them of the church's prayerful support, allows better accountability to the church, and gives the missionaries a greater sense of security and reassurance during hard times on the field. The church in Antioch separated Paul, Barnabas, and Mark to disciple the nations with much prayer and fasting. This must separate the workers for church planting in another field not only physically but also emotionally--from their home church, family, mission base, or friends. Some organizations practice frequent laying on of hands for blessing and power for ministry. In this case, the separation ceremony may not be very meaningful if all you do is lay on hands again. You make it special, so that all involved know that the apostles ("sent ones") have truly been sent by the body through the power of God's Spirit. Perhaps that is why the church in Antioch fasted first (Acts 13:1-3).

ARRANGE TO MOBILIZE THE FOLLOWING CATEGORIES OF PEOPLE OR GROUPS ON THE FIELD:

☐ **The new national church.**

Envision a national church in a currently unreached field, obeying Jesus' commands and therefore reproducing--often in tiny house churches--among its own people (Matt. 28:18-20). Wise mission planners, like military strategists, begin with long-range objectives stated so clearly that each preparatory step is self-evident. In planning for a specific unreached field, they keep its limited resources or freedom in mind and reason backward through preparatory steps, avoiding programs too expensive or too electronic for national churches to reproduce. *But first, we prepare the right kind of:*

☐ **Key regional leaders (national *pastors of pastors*).**

For widespread church reproduction, new servant leaders on the regional (synod) level mobilize other pastors--a skill acquired from disciplers who take personal, loving responsibility for the fruitful ministry of others, otherwise they become grasping and demanding. *But first we develop the right kind of:*

☐ **National pastors/elders.**

Good pastors mobilize others for ministry (Eph. 4:11-16)--a skill acquired on the job, not in classrooms. *But first we must properly train:*

☐ **Potential national leaders who are servants, shepherds, and mobilizers.**

Pastoral students are not simply educated but are trained to edify and mobilize the local body of Christ (Eph. 4:11-16). In most fields, this happens best in churches where trainers harmonize their teaching with other gifts (1 Cor. 12-13). Remember: balanced discipling relates the Word to the work in love--teaching in love to mobilize our disciples to do God's work. In most pioneer fields formal institutional training is impractical. Elder types cannot leave their responsibilities. Economically motivated youths respond but, lacking preparatory education, cannot assimilate the intensive input and, lacking models of well-established churches, cannot realistically apply it. *But first we lay a discipleship foundation with:*

☐ **New Christians.**

We teach believers before all else to obey Jesus' commands (Matt. 28:19-20)--believe, repent, be baptized and receive the Holy Spirit, love, break bread, pray, give, and disciple others (Acts 2:38-47). Prolonged indoctrination before loving obedience stifles the sacrificial discipleship and makes it harder to mobilize one for ministry. We help new believers to see themselves as highly disciplined pilgrims in search of a better country. The journey is difficult but exhilarating. What a privilege to labor in Jesus' Kingdom; what joy! We were created--and re-created--for this! We help brand new believers to find real joy in serving our King. This joy of serving is not reserved for some elite group in the Kingdom (e.g., full-time clergy). Every child of God is enlisted in God's army to wage warfare--and not as volunteers in an auxiliary branch of the army when they feel like it, leaving the "real work" to the clergy of the regular army. Even George Washington found that such an army could not win a war. When we are conscripted into this army, we find a whole new discipline; our whole life is changed. *But first we establish the type of relationship that loving discipling can build on, with:*

☐ **Pre-Christians.**

We let the converts see the crucified and risen Christ living in us (2 Cor. 5:15)--the full, sacrificial, abundant, pilgrim life lived out in a hostile world. They see us modeling the loving relationships needed for further discipling and witnessing of Jesus' saving death and resurrection in a way they can imitate lovingly with their family and friends. *But first we form a church planting team skilled in such discipling methods, for both new Christians and leaders:*

☐ **The team entering the target field.**

Teams, then, not only combine the needed gifts and cooperative spirit but screen out technology, equipment, and methods that nationals cannot imitate, afford, or pass on. *But first we may need:*

☐ **Missionaries from the two-thirds world.**

We might become partners with emerging churches that are now mobilizing their own foreign missionaries, who relate better to many unreached peoples. No amount of training to adapt to a new culture equals being born culturally close--that is, having similar politics, race, language, economic and education levels, family size, rural/urban life-style, and world view. *But first we deal with:*

☐ **Bi-vocational missionaries.**

Only bi-vocational missionaries can reside in most of the remaining unreached fields long enough for church multiplication. They need, like Paul, cross-cultural church planting experience, teams, formal commissioning (Acts 13:1-3), and employment such as a small business that puts them with the working class.

HELP CHURCH MULTIPLIERS EVALUATE THEIR USE OF MINISTRY TIME.

Let us manage our limited time in a way that honors God. Reproductive evangelism and church planting take enormous amounts of time. To establish priorities daily and over the years, we keep in mind Jesus' explicit commands and our God-given priorities (Eph. 5.15-17). Christian workers use their time better if they do the following:

Delegate pastoral and evangelistic responsibilities to other leaders. **Let members do things; once someone agrees to do something, avoid overcontrol of his or her work. Do not use your wife (or husband) merely to run errands unless that is the role you both have agreed upon for her (or him).**

Give your family ample time each day, and a whole day (on the average) per week. Take your Sabbaths (there was a time when you might have been stoned to death if you didn't)! Do not allow your family to feel that they have to compete for your time.

Discuss your ministry regularly with your spouse and children so that they appreciate it and do not begrudge the time you must spend away from them. Talk and pray with them about your plans (and theirs) before you go on a trip and review with them what happened (to them, too) when you return.

Avoid arguing with skeptics. New missionaries, desperately seeking for contacts, often cast their pearls before swine. We may enjoy an occasional friendly theological argument, but we must not get caught up in controversial issues. We discipline ourselves to avoid non-edifying details of theological discussions (remember Paul's warnings about foolish questions and genealogies; see 1 Tim. 1:4; Titus 3:9). Sometimes we cannot avoid a controversy. But we can avoid giving it too much time; keep doing the positive things you know God wants you to do. Don't feel you always have to prove yourself right. (It is dangerous for a human always to be right.)

Start immediately turning over long-range leadership responsibilities to local leaders.

Train continually those adults who are potential leaders; give them responsibilities as soon as they are ready.

Keep analyzing how you have been spending your time.

Be ruthless in cutting out of your agenda all activities--no matter how enjoyable--that do not move you measurably toward your God-given goals. Avoid too much television or other forms of entertainment that do not edify or unite your family.

Have another person monitor your progress. No one effectively evaluates the use of his or her own time; we all need someone to help us.

If you are a hard-working husband, have another person--preferably your wife--schedule your appointments. Does your wife feel insecure at times because of your time commitments? Does she (or the children) need to compete with the Lord's work for your attention? If you are unsure, then they probably do--ask her about it! If the answer is yes, then authorize her to schedule your time, especially for activities that take you away from your home overnight or longer. If you often feel pressured, driven by guilt to have to fill every half hour of your time with work, you are taking on too many responsibilities; some of the things you are doing are not God's will. Give your wife authority to schedule regular sabbaths (the equivalent of one day a week spent with the family, when your mind is not on the work). During another week, make up for special events that would cause undue hardship if missed.

Start managing your time right now, by recording your plans to do so. Pray for daily self-discipline to follow God's priorities.

☐ **Develop Reproductive Organization.** With love born of the Holy Spirit, you and your disciples should be able to organize the body of Christ to help it to reproduce, by doing the following things. Mark those you expect to give attention:

☐ **If you are a missionary from the outside, disciple potential national leaders as you build up the growing body of Christ through them.** Do not try to do all the teaching, pastoring, and decision-making yourself; model it, then step back and let your own "Timothy" do the work. Enable many others to begin teaching and shepherding in their own homes. Provide Bible reading schedules for these proto-leaders to use to teach in their homes and in small groups modeled after the family. Set up discipleship "chains" (you teach one of the men, and he in turn teaches others). For example, help your "Timothy" set up a regular time of Bible study in his home, then encourage him to help another newer man do the same in his home. These two links in a discipleship chain will often keep multiplying. New churches often suffer and fail from "one link" discipling chains, which involve no multiplication. All the believers are linked directly to one overworked church planter. They watch the church planter do all the discipling until he collapses from exhaustion.

☐ **Disciple able, mature men (elder types).** Avoid training single, young men in pioneer fields as pastors. Train men who qualify better as "elders" (or shepherds; see Titus 1:5-9). In a pioneer field it is hard to find men who meet all the requirements, so we train the best ones that God gives us, using the Bible's guidelines as our criteria. Remember, they must be able to teach others. As a general rule, new churches in pioneer fields where there are no experienced pastoral leaders or elders yet get along better if led by several provisional elders. They are provisional in the sense that they are too new to be considered permanent elders or pastors. (Notice Acts 14:23, where Paul named fairly new believers as elders, for new churches in a pioneer field.)

ORGANIZE FOR CHURCH MULTIPLICATION

☐ **Organize after--not before--you know exactly what you will do.**
Avoid detailed rules and bylaws until they are obviously needed; discard them as soon as they are no longer necessary. We need to have our goal fixed on the horizon, but also to keep developing the path as we go along. We constantly evaluate our progress as we work toward the goal, but we also allow for real breakthroughs when progress seems to be blocked. This forces us to explore new ways around the obstacles. As Scoggins puts it, "We have found, in our experience with house churches, that such `horizon travel' leaves plenty of room for innovation, new initiatives, and a great deal of looking to the Lord!"

☐ **Avoid placing new workers in an area simply because there is a "need."**
Let them minister in a situation that maximizes their gifts and talents, not simply to keep the organization or mere programs functioning smoothly. Failure to do this is a common error of mission agency field supervisors and results in many missionaries "washing out" or "burning out" unnecessarily.

☐ **Apply the biblical pattern of organization: namely, cooperation among those with different gifts.**
The Western, secular, institutional pattern of specialization separates persons with different gifts or ministries, forming independent and often competitive commissions, departments, or branches. This type of organization very often stifles church reproduction. We help people with divergent gifts to find ways to cooperate, ways that open new vistas for effective ministry. The people in a team or in a church needs a vision for what they believe God desires them to accomplish through their gifts. Once a vision is established, each person needs to find his or her place in accomplishing it. Remember "horizon travel." As people are added, the vision will need fine-tuning as each one brings his or her special gift to bear. Over time, the vision will change as we travel from one horizon to the next; God does not let us see the entire future but leads us from one phase to another.

☐ **Enable volunteer workers to set their own goals and performance standards.**

The underlying motive for all true Christian service is love for Jesus, who said, "If you love me, obey my commands" (John 14:15). Once this discipling mentality of loving obedience is established in the entire body, help volunteer workers to visualize and achieve what God wants them to do, out of love and self-initiative, rather than pushing them, offering rewards, threatening, using organizational clout or competition (remember that competition, in the sense of rivalry, is condemned in Scripture).

☐ **Have gifted shepherds with a servant's heart make crucial decisions for a church or group, as taught in 1 Peter 5:1-5 and Hebrew 13:17.**

Do not rely on majority rule (except in matters requiring a congregational vote for legal reasons). Scripture and history show that the majority seldom vote for the cross-bearing, faith-stretching disciple's route; they typically choose the more secure, traditional, least demanding route. The Kingdom of God on earth (the church) is not a democracy but a monarchy. Reproductive discipling requires loving authority, in which the strong leader is a humble servant of all (Matt. 20:25-28). Many sound discipling programs have been scrapped because their participants submitted to the majority rule within their church or denomination. Let Jesus be our King!

☐ **Develop body life between new churches and groups.**

Church multiplication thrives on loving relationships between churches. Scripture reveals nothing of the independent spirit that some American missionaries impart to a new church. They mean well, but they are from a culture that idealizes individualism and personal rights above the rights of the society. Scoggins relates:

> We set up "fellowships" of house churches. Each fellowship is a network of from two to six cooperating house churches. The leaders meet together regularly for fellowship, training, counsel, and discussion of decisions that might affect the other house churches in the fellowship. The congregations all meet together, usually monthly. The relationships established between the leaders help in preventing a congregation from developing ingrown or "cultic" devotion to a strong leader, as well as enabling older elders to mentor younger ones. These congregational relationships reduce the number of failures of the house churches.

The New Testament consistently emphasizes developing loving, cooperative, edifying body life between churches or groups of believers. Christ's body is not a local congregation, although that is where practice of loving unity starts, among persons with different gifts and interests. For example, when the persecution started in apostolic times, the primitive churches in Jerusalem and Ephesus became clusters of closely knit, cooperating house churches. Their organization, like that of modern churches in highly restricted fields, resembled an underground crime network. In restricted fields we do not form large congregations, but an underground network of tiny house churches.

☐ **Trust the Holy Spirit to motivate new leaders.**

Do not fear that false doctrine will automatically creep into rapidly reproducing groups or churches. History proves the opposite. Healthy, normally reproductive churches or cell groups are loyal to their disciplers and are oriented to obedience to Christ; false doctrine seldom is a problem. In contrast, churches that are overprotected by foreign leaders who are suspicious of false doctrine creeping in every time they turn their backs provoke a rebellious spirit that opens the window for all kinds of rare birds to fly in.

☐ **Do not fear to encourage a new leader simply because he has weaknesses--build on his strengths.**

Trusting the Holy Spirit, we build on what a potential leader can do; we release him to do it, instead of building rules around him to make him "safe." David was a great leader because God built on his strengths, not his obvious weaknesses. Especially in a pioneer field, use the best men that God gives you. There is no perfect leader. Scoggins emphasizes:

> In our experience, strong men have strong weaknesses. If we develop good relationships between the leaders

of a church, God uses other elders to offset those weaknesses, so that the strong leader does not become independent and proud but rather sees his need for his fellow elders. Whether serving on a team or in a house church fellowship, the leaders need to set the pace in relying on others to help us in our weaknesses. As we become more aware of our own weaknesses, we become more willing to mobilize other leaders with glaring weaknesses. We find more and more frequently that we need to rely on their strengths!

☐ **Delegate pastoral responsibilities.**

Let men with pastoral potential develop their gifts. Model pastoral skills for them. Give them the tools to study the Bible to teach its truths to others, especially the ability to do inductive Bible study. Help them to lead disciples at all levels to multiply themselves and their church or group.

☐ **Help each potential pastor to clarify personal objectives.**

Enable him to define his God-given goals and the little, intermediate steps he needs to keep moving toward them.

☐ **Evaluate your progress by measuring results, not efforts.**

Define goals in terms of concrete results expected. Help the leaders of each team, group, or church to evaluate its progress in terms of such God-given results. Measuring efforts does not tell you if you are progressing toward your goals. By efforts we mean the things we do to win people for Christ and edify the church (meetings, classes, lessons, reading, programs, crusades, etc.). By concrete results we mean converts baptized, new churches born, new classes started, daily prayer and regular, sacrificial giving begun by families, new disciples mobilized for ministry, new Bible studies *begun* (the on-going classes themselves are efforts), and transformation of lives and families. In short, loving obedience leads to *efforts* made in the power of the Holy Spirit, which lead to *results*. This chain of cause and effect cannot be short-circuited.

☐ **If in a pioneer field, use a simple form of worship service that new leaders with limited training can imitate and pass on at once to others they train.**

Use a worship style that new elders can lead themselves with a minimum of supervision, one that is culturally relevant. For example, if they are new believers, they should not do pulpit oratory; it will make them proud. They should celebrate the Lord's Supper weekly, read Scripture, exhort, and tell Bible stories that their disciplers have helped them prepare.

☐ **Develop a midwife mentality for reproducing churches.**

Especially if your church planting team is working cross-culturally, you are there to help those in the other culture reproduce on their own initiative in the power of the Holy Spirit. We do not cause the reproduction ourselves. The new congregation should take all responsibility as soon as possible for giving birth to still other churches and training their pastors. The stronger the team itself is organizationally, the harder it is sometimes to keep its hands off the new church and let the infant church take initiative in the power of the Holy Spirit.

☐ **Accept accountability only to a leader who encourages you in a ministry that makes use of your gifts and strengths, in fulfillment of what God is calling you to do.**

Again, prayerfully verify a potential field supervisor's attitude before committing your life's career to an organization, church, or team.

☐ **Become experts in discipling on all levels: with pre-Christians, new Christians, older Christians, and leaders.**

Most of the world's remaining unreached fields need church planters and evangelists skilled in personal discipling. In Muslim, Communist, and other restricted and unchurched fields where Christian gatherings are prohibited—which represent one-third of the world's people—missionaries must work without classrooms or pulpits. A church that practices biblical discipling does not need a special evangelism program or department. Evangelism is integrated into every aspect of the church's life, just as Paul includes it in the normal work of a pastor (2 Tim. 4:1-5).

About time we got
toward the end.
My wings are growing
weary.

APPENDIX D. An Example of an Activity Review File for a Sending Church

(New Hope Community Church, Cucamonga, Calif.)

ACTIVITIES FOR A MISSION ACTION GROUP

Activities for a mission action group to mobilize a church as a body for global outreach. Mark those which apply:

Preparing for a Mission Action Group

☐ Prayerfully seek authorization by the elders or leaders of the church, and the support of the senior pastor, for such an action group.

☐ Arrange accountability of the Mission Action Group to the church leadership.

☐ Recruit committed volunteers for the Mission Action Group.

Aim for at least one group representative from each department, class, ministry, or small group in the church. They take information, prayer requests, and reports of needs to their groups so that the entire church body is involved. Do not allow the church to polarize around two parties: those who believe in foreign missions and those who are indifferent.

Mobilizing the Mission Action Group

☐ Orient mission action group volunteers to their individual tasks.

Help volunteers with their job descriptions and arrange accountability for each one. Their orientation may include audiovisual aids or skits, and prayer for the vision.

☐ Arrange for the group to meet monthly to plan, report work done, evaluate, pray, and strategize.

☐ Help each mission action group worker to communicate in a way that relates to the age, spiritual maturity, and nature of the worker's department or group.

For example, a worker with children might tell stories, another with teenagers might arrange mission awareness projects and field trips.

☐ See that group workers mobilize their respective groups to do the activity designated for each month.

Meet personally with those who need special help, especially to get started.

Other Possible Mission Action Group Activities

☐ Catalog available resources for mission awareness and mobilization.

Keep a tab on tools for increasing mission awareness and mobilizing volunteer workers.

☐ Network with other churches that are mobilizing for mission work.

Share with these churches ideas and resources; encourage and pray for each other.

☐ Develop a working relationship with mission agencies and missionary training institutions that are supportive of your church's program.

Group or Class Activities for a *Twelve-Month Cycle:*

☐ Month 1: **Arrange for informed prayer by each department or group** (use *Global Prayer Digest*).

☐ Month 2: **Teach a comprehensive biblical perspective.**

Use Old and New Testament passages on God's plan for the nations (use related sections in the Perspectives on the World Christian Movement).

☐ Month 3: **Arrange for giving by each department or group.**

☐ Month 4: **Present a comprehensive historical survey.**

Investigate what God has been doing throughout the history of his church to extend his kingdom on earth (Use Tucker's *From Jerusalem to Irian Jaya*).

☐ Month 5: **Arrange for local mission work.**

☐ Month 6: **Heighten awareness of worldwide mission work** (Use *Target Earth* and Johnson's *Operation World*, William Carey Library, Pasadena).

☐ Month 7: **Arrange for effective mission ministry career counseling** (use the *Perspectives Ministry Career Guide*, William Carey Library, Pasadena).

☐ Month 8: **Review the past and current mission outreach of your own church.**

☐ Month 9: **Arrange for effective training for mission work.**

Find what further training is needed by career and volunteer mission workers. Provide for potential missionaries to receive training in programs that use models that are transferable to their target culture (review section D, *Perspectives Ministry Career Guide*).

☐ Month 10: **Impart a cultural orientation for global outreach.**

Help each department or group to appreciate other cultures and God's love for the nations with their distinctive cultures (use related sections in *Perspectives on the World Christian Movement*).

☐ Month 11: **Plan and pray for the church to reproduce daughter and granddaughter churches at home and abroad**

(Review this *Church Multiplication Guide* with team members).

☐ Month 12: **Mobilize and commission a missionary team**

(Use George Miley's *Antioch Network Papers*, 7854 Nichals St., Lemon Grove, CA 91945).

Appendix E, Items to Review

Mark below in the *first box* □ items you will review, discuss or plan with your coworkers. Mark the *second box* when they are being practiced. Add plans to your *Activity Review Files* under the corresponding ministry activities. The numbers beside the items below correspond to the item subtitles in bold face in the text, *not to page numbers*.

Introduction

□□ 1. The simplicity of church multiplication (trust in Gods power).
□□ 2. Keep in mind your ministry, and that of your co-workers, as you use this Guide.
□□ 3. Use this Guide to train others in a church context.
□□ 4. Develop Activity Review Files.
□□ 5. Depending on your ministry, you may want to prepare more than one of the following types of Activity Review Files
□□ 6. Suggested Reading
□□ 7. Describe how you will record and review with your co-workers the activity plans you note as you read this *Guide*.

Chapter 1, The Need for Total Obedience

□□ 8. Commit yourself to obey Jesus' specific commands before and above all else.
□□ 9. Make disciples who before all else obey Jesus' basic commands.
□□ 10. Measure growth in Christ by each person's obedience to him, in order to disciple as he commands.
□□ 11. Discern human policies as temporary and of secondary importance, to avoid rules or policies that stifle multiplication.
□□ 12. For the kind of discipling that reproduces, help members learn to discern Jesus' commands.
□□ 13. Your plans for your people to obey the basic commands of Christ in simple, childlike faith and love.

Chapter 2. Obeying Jesus' Command to Repent, Believe, and Receive the Holy Spirit

□□ 14. Do simply what Jesus commands to do to be saved--repent and believe.
□□ 15. Witness as the apostles did, to bring about faith and repentance.
□□ 16. Your plans in response to Jesus' command to repent, believe and receive the Holy Spirit.

Chapter 3. Obeying Jesus' Command to Baptize

□□ 17. For converts to be born from the very beginning as obedient disciples, confirm salvation with baptism without delay.
□□ 18. Help converts to trust the Holy Spirit to unite them to Jesus and sense His presence, through their baptism
□□ 19. Your plans in response to Jesus' command to baptize; later, with your co-workers.

Chapter 4. Obeying Jesus' Command to Make Disciples

□□ 20. Teach new believers immediately the full meaning of discipleship.
□□ 21. To assure continued reproduction, help converts who are still outside the church to become obedient, corporate disciples.
□□ 22. Relate the Word to life and ministry, just as Jesus and his apostles modeled in their teaching.
□□ 23. To assure continued church reproduction, disciple on all levels of Christian maturity.
□□ 24. To mobilize men and women for ministry, teach with loving authority.
□□ 25. To reproduce churches in a pioneer field, integrate church planting with pastoral training.
□□ 26. Help a convert teach the Word to his family.
□□ 27. Your general plans for discipling.

Chapter 5. Obeying Jesus' Command to Love

□□ 28. Enable potential leaders to develop their own ministries without fearing those who are over them.
□□ 29. Start from the beginning to disciple a new believer with love and personal interest.
□□ 30. Help new believers immediately to care for the needy.
□□ 31. In poverty areas, combine church planting with community development.
□□ 32. For continued, healthy church reproduction, let the Holy Spirit harmonize the use of different spiritual gifts in love.
□□ 33. To discover and develop spiritual gifts, release potential leaders to work with new churches and small groups.
□□ 34. Detect and care for personal or family needs in small, loving groups.
□□ 35. For organization that reproduces, do balanced discipling.
□□ 36. Your plans for your people to disciple others with genuine love, including for training leaders.

Chapter 6. Obeying Jesus' Command to Break Bread

☐☐ 37. Glorify Jesus Christ by remembering Him with the ceremony He gave us.
☐☐ 38. Avoid excessive fear of allowing too much--or too little--of the mystery in Communion services.
☐☐ 39. Invite the Holy Spirit to work powerfully through this ceremony that Jesus instituted.
☐☐ 40. To bless God and receive his blessing, practice all vital parts of worship.
☐☐ 41. Use the spiritual gifts that God gives to certain people to help others praise him in a way that pleases him and blesses us.
☐☐ 42. For more effective worship and evangelism, deal conscientiously with special seasons and holidays.
☐☐ 43. Your plans related to Communion.

Chapter 7. Obeying Jesus' Command to Pray

☐☐ 44. Pray constantly for God's enablement to keep reproducing as a church.
☐☐ 45. Help your disciples to grow spiritually by developing their daily personal and family devotional life.
☐☐ 46. Pray continually for the salvation of the lost and for a vision of normal church reproduction.
☐☐ 47. Plan prayerfully for continued growth and reproduction.
☐☐ 48. In keeping with the vision for ongoing growth and multiplication, continually reproduce new leaders.
☐☐ 49. You plans to prayerfully tap God's power to grow and reproduce.

Chapter 8. Obeying Jesus' Command to Give

☐☐ 50. To help converts escape the misery of severe poverty, teach them sacrificial, voluntary stewardship from the beginning.
☐☐ 51. To avoid dependency or resentment, fund church planting in poverty areas with extreme care.
☐☐ 53. Your plans for the churches to practice Christian stewardship and support their own workers.

Chapter 9. The Viewpoint of the Pre-Christian

☐☐ 54. Prayerfully plan for a movement of the people for Christ.
☐☐ 55. Do incarnational evangelism.
☐☐ 56. Develop a doctrinal foundation for witnessing so that converts are converted to Jesus Christ and not just to the church.
☐☐ 57 Practice reproductive witnessing so that converts hear the gospel in a way that they can pass on immediately to others.
☐☐ 58. Communicate first the essentials of the gospel.
☐☐ 59. Pray regularly and fervently for those we witness to.
☐☐ 60. Befriend and win the confidence of respected heads of households.
☐☐ 61. Help heads of households to evangelize their families and friends.
☐☐ 62. In a new community share the gospel first with a person of peace (Luke 10:6).
☐☐ 63. Form a new church or group inside this circle of friends and relatives.
☐☐ 64. Where meeting in large groups is illegal, form several tiny groups that can more easily avoid detection by authorities.
☐☐ 65. Give ample time for the Holy Spirit to convince a family.
☐☐ 66. Help the head of a family to affirm verbally the essential gospel truths during each presentation of the gospel.
☐☐ 67. Do not push people into making crisis decisions in the Western sense.
☐☐ 68. Do not count converts until they are added to a church, by baptism, that obeys the Lord's basic commands in love.
☐☐ 69. Start with the basic stories of redemption.
☐☐ 70. Help unconverted heads of families and other natural leaders to communicate the gospel to their own families and friends.
☐☐ 71. Get everyone to talking about the gospel on the streets, in the bars, at work--everywhere.
☐☐ 72. Use methods that are easily imitated at once by those you train.
☐☐ 73. Use the Old Testament, too.
☐☐ 74. Follow up conversion with baptism as soon as possible.
☐☐ 75. Assure each convert of the church's loving acceptance at once.
☐☐ 76. Your plans to deal with pre-Christians in a way that allows God's Holy Spirit to convince them of their need for forgiveness.

Chapter 10. The Viewpoint of the Evangelist

☐☐ 77. Aim at more than mere decisions.
☐☐ 78. If working with a cross-cultural church planting team, give preference to unevangelized fields.
☐☐ 79. Strengthen the gift of the evangelists by bringing their proclamation in line with the apostles' emphasis.
☐☐ 80. Use the ''keys'' for anointed witnessing.
☐☐ 81. Where people are hostile against converting, allow converts to make their own decisions as to how they will testify.
☐☐ 82. Your plans to do the work of an evangelist.

Chapter 11. The Viewpoint of the Church Multiplication Team

☐☐ 83. If you lead a team starting a new church or group, prepare an Activity Review File for a new church or group to follow.
☐☐ 84. Imitate the outreach and witness of the apostles' church planting teams.
☐☐ 85. Eliminate a major cause of missionary failure and burnout by deploying church-based teams.
☐☐ 86. To avoid tensions in the home, help married church planters to define the wife's role in ministry.
☐☐ 87. If you are a team leader, help your members to agree that the church planting team is temporary in any one locale.
☐☐ 89. Appreciate the differences in another culture, especially if you are entering a pioneer field.
☐☐ 92. Arrange on-the-job training, if needed, for team members from another country or ethnic group.
☐☐ 93. Target a responsive segment of the population.
☐☐ 94. Help national leaders to take full pastoral responsibility as soon as possible.
☐☐ 95. Once churches are multiplying, avoid burnout by turning over problems to the new elders, and moving to new areas.
☐☐ 96. Recruit team members committed to seeing the job through.
☐☐ 97. Filter out non-essentials.
☐☐ 98. Select team members who meet the requirements of your specific field and ministry.
☐☐ 99. Plan the essential activities for a church multiplication team.
☐☐ 100. Your plans to mobilize church multiplication teams.

Chapter 12. The Viewpoint of the Field Supervisor

☐☐ 101. Help those with the apostolic gift to select their field wisely.
☐☐ 102. Take advantage of the brutal class discrimination in most resistant fields (but avoid messy foreign politics).
☐☐ 103. Help team members to bond with their people.
☐☐ 104. To keep everyone working in loving harmony, personally disciple others just as Jesus commanded and modeled it.
☐☐ 105. Disciple new leaders in another culture the way Jesus and his apostles modeled discipling.
☐☐ 106. Launch a team for a distant field with a separation ceremony.
☐☐ 107. Do strategic planning, to mobilize different types of people on the field.
☐☐ 108. Help your workers evaluate their use of ministry time.
☐☐ 109. Make practical plans now for reproductive organization
☐☐ 110. Your plans for reproductive organization and servant leadership.

Chapter 13. The Viewpoint of the Small Group

☐☐ 111. Plan activities now to enable reproductive discipleship in small groups or cells.
☐☐ 112. Make plans now to enable the birth of small groups, or of churches that start as small groups or cells.
☐☐ 113. Your plans for small group leaders to reproduce themselves in new leaders of new groups or house churches.

Chapter 14. The Viewpoint of the House Church

☐☐ 114. Verify the circumstances that normally show when house churches are needed.
☐☐ 115. Be content with being a house church if that is how God is leading.
☐☐ 116. To keep multiplying, prepare new house church leaders as on-the-job apprentices.
☐☐ 117. Take advantage of the small group atmosphere to enable entire families to participate in worship.
☐☐ 118. Discern positive, objective indications of the need to multiply house churches rather than erect, expand or rent a building.
☐☐ 119. Discern danger signs warning that one ever-growing church centered in a building is stifling freedom in the Spirit.
☐☐ 120. In new or embryonic churches gear most of the Bible teaching to building relationships between members and leaders.
☐☐ 121. Once a new group decides to become a house church, affirm the commitment with a serious, positive covenant.
☐☐ 122. Form small "gathering meetings" for unbelievers, led by the converts themselves.
☐☐ 123. Form a cluster of churches, with "servant-leaders" in each church, who also coordinate cooperation between churches.
☐☐ 124. Your general plans for house churches.

Chapter 15. The Viewpoint of the Mother Church, or Sending Body

☐☐ 125. Mobilize those in your church to whom God gives the apostolic gift as *teams*.
☐☐ 126. Let your church's overseas reproduction continue freely without tying it to any limiting factors.
☐☐ 127. Provide unbiased career counseling.
☐☐ 128. Help team members to love and appreciate the church and to know exactly what they are reproducing.
☐☐ 129. Pray for coworkers to rely on your church's God-given power to grow by multiplication as well as by addition.
☐☐ 130. Give missionary candidates experience in effective witnessing.
☐☐ 131. Seek cross-cultural apostles who are committed to go and multiply churches.
☐☐ 132. List activities to help an established church reproduce.
☐☐ 133. Your general plans for your sending church multiplication teams.

Chapter 16. The Viewpoint of the Trainer of Pastors or Missionaries

☐☐ 134. To impart church multiplication skills, train pastors/elders and church planters on the job.

☐☐ 135. To keep new churches multiplying where there are no experienced leaders, name provisional elders.

☐☐ 136. Continually relate the doctrine (the Word of God) to the student's current practice (the work of God) as you teach.

☐☐ 137. Use formal residential theological education where conditions exist that warrant it.

☐☐ 138. Use the gift of teaching to edify (build up) the church, not just to educate a student.

☐☐ 140. Learn to disciple other leaders by being discipled.

☐☐ 142. Help your pastoral disciples to keep reproducing other disciples.

☐☐ 143. Help all who participate in the development of leaders to make the commitments needed for church multiplication.

☐☐ 144. Use biblical methods for discipling leaders.

☐☐ 145. In each teaching session, respond to your student's needs.

☐☐ 146. Require pastoral students to be active corporate disciples during their training by working in a pastoral ministry.

☐☐ 147. Carefully relate reading to the practical work.

☐☐ 148. Use materials that are geared to the trainees' level of education, to their needs, and to personal discipling.

☐☐ 149. Continually and ruthlessly evaluate the results of your teaching.

☐☐ 150. Be creative in communicating God's Word.

☐☐ 151. Model all pastoral, evangelistic, and church planting skills as you train pastors.

☐☐ 152. Use equipment that is available to those who imitate your methods.

☐☐ 153. If you need to hone the skill of discipling pastors, enlist one or more persons who are good models to disciple you.

☐☐ 154. Do not model skills or methods rooted in the paganism of your own culture.

☐☐ 155. Develop personal, edifying, long-term relationships with your pastoral students.

☐☐ 156. Supplement personal discipling with large group teaching when possible.

☐☐ 157. To deal with ministry details, separate disciples of different levels.

☐☐ 158. Mark what applies to your ministry, among the following Helps for Combining Doctrine and Duty:

☐☐ 159. Your plans for training.

Chapter 17. The Viewpoint of the Church Leader

☐☐ 160. For reproductive discipling, mobilize every member--young and old--of your congregation for gift-based ministry.

☐☐ 161. First determine what God wants your people to do; only then organize for it.

☐☐ 162. Review the ministries of your church(es) periodically to verify continued practice of those things that are essential.

☐☐ 163. Your plans for your church activities.

Chapter 18. The Viewpoint of the Mission Career Counselor

☐☐ 164. Provide unbiased career counseling.

☐☐ 165. Review your church's mission activity periodically, keeping in mind the entire scope of mission mobilization.

☐☐ 166. Help leaders of a sending church to plan and arrange for needed training and orientation.

☐☐ 167. Mobilize people for these ministries through their love for Jesus.

☐☐ 178. Your plans for mission career counseling.

Appendices

☐☐ **Appendix A**. An example of a personal Activity Review Chart.

☐☐ **Appendix B**. An example of an Activity Review File for a new church.

☐☐ **Appendix C**. An Activity Review File for a church multiplication team (for *starting a new church, separating a team, mobilizing eight categories of people on the field, time management* and *organizing for multiplication*).

☐☐ **Appendix D**. An example of an Activity Review File for a sending church.

☐☐ **Appendix E**. Review items (this same list)